Active Experiences for Active Children

SCIENCE

Carol Seefeldt
Alice Galper

Merrill
Prentice Hall

Upper Saddle River, New Jersey
Columbus, Ohio

Library of Congress Cataloging in Publication Data

Seefeldt, Carol.
    Active experiences for active children. Science / Carol Seefeldt, Alice Galper.
        p. cm.
    Includes bibliographical references and index.
    ISBN 0-13-083433-5 (pbk.)
        1. Science—Study and teaching (Early childhood)—Activity programs. I. Galper, Alice.
    II. Title.

LB1139.5.S35 S44 2002
372.3'5044—dc21   2001037068

Vice President and Publisher: Jeffery W. Johnston
Executive Editor: Ann Castel Davis
Editorial Assistant: Keli Gemrich
Production Editor: Sheryl Glicker Langner
Design Coordinator: Diane C. Lorenzo
Photo Coordinator: Sandy Lenahan
Cover Designer: Thomas Borah
Cover Photo: Corbis/The Stock Market
Production Manager: Laura Messerly
Director of Marketing: Kevin Flanagan
Marketing Manager: Amy June
Marketing Coordinator: Barbara Koontz

This book was set in Times Roman and Frutiger by Carlisle Communications, Ltd. It was printed and bound by Courier Kendallville, Inc. The cover was printed by The Lehigh Press, Inc.

Photo Credits: pp. 3, 79 by John Paul Endress/Silver Burdett Ginn; pp. 9, 49 by Laima E. Druskis/Prentice Hall College; p. 21 by Timothy P. Dingman/Prentice Hall College; p. 29 by Marc Anderson/Prentice Hall College; p. 39 courtesy of Prentice Hall; p. 65 by Todd Yarrington/Merrill; p. 87 by Barbara Schwartz/Merrill; p. 95 by Anne Vega/Merrill; p. 107 by Anthony Magnacca/Merrill; p. 119 by Andy Brunk/Merrill; p. 133 by Scott Cunningham/Merrill.

Pearson Education Ltd., *London*
Pearson Education Australia Pty. Limited, *Sydney*
Pearson Education Singapore, Pte. Ltd.
Pearson Education North Asia Ltd., *Hong Kong*
Pearson Education Canada, Ltd., *Toronto*
Pearson Educación de Mexico, S.A. de C.V.
Pearson Education—Japan, *Tokyo*
Pearson Education Malaysia, Pte. Ltd.
Pearson Education, *Upper Saddle River, New Jersey*

10 9 8 7 6 5 4 3 2 1
ISBN: 0-13-083433-5

◆ This book is dedicated to Ann Davis, editor extraordinaire.

Preface

"What can I do tomorrow?" teachers ask. "I've run out of ideas. And I don't mean just another silly activity. I need something that will keep children involved and lead to successful learning." Grounded in John Dewey's philosophy that all genuine education comes through experience, but that not all experiences are equally educative, *Active Experiences for Active Children: Science* answers teachers' questions about what to do tomorrow and on into the school year.

Both pre- and in-service teachers will find this book useful. It is suitable as a text, or a supplemental text, for early childhood courses in community colleges and four-year college programs. The experiences in this book would provide a basis for a series of workshops or short courses in science for children.

There are numerous activity books available. These, however, present isolated science activities that are often meaningless to children and void of any real content or learning. *Active Experiences for Active Children: Science* offers teachers an integrated approach to planning science learning for young children.

Its practicality will also be ideal for teachers who desire the best for young children but have limited training or formal preparation for teaching science. Professionals working in childcare, Head Start, or other early childhood settings will find that *Active Experiences for Active Children: Science* supports their growth and understanding of how to put theory into practice.

ORGANIZATION

This book is the third in a series of books designed to illustrate how to plan and implement meaningful, thematic experiences that truly educate young children instead of just keeping them busy. Teachers are given guides to planning and implementing curriculum that will lead to children's academic success using developmentally appropriate methods for teaching science.

Active Experiences for Active Children: Science consists of clear, concise, and usable guides for planning meaningful science content and teaching strategies for children in childcare, preschool, Head Start, or other early educational programs. Experiences are expanded into the early primary grades.

The experiences in this book lead to successful science learning because they

- Are grounded in children's interests and needs in their here-and-now world.

- Have integrity in terms of content key to science learning.

- Involve children in group work, investigations, and projects.

- Have continuity. One experience builds on another, forming a complete, coherent, integrated learning curriculum for young children as well as connecting the early childhood setting to children's homes and communities.

- Provide time and opportunity for children to think and reflect on their experiences.

- Contain a large number of resources (books, Web sites, magazines, audios, and visuals) for both teachers and children.

The first five chapters describe the foundation for planning and implementing experiential science learning. These offer pre- and in-service teachers of young children an overview of theory and research based upon Dewey, the constructivist view of children's learning, and the latest guidelines proposed for the science curriculum. The first chapter illustrates how theories of learning and teaching can be put into practice. This is followed by two chapters on indoor and outdoor environments for science. Next the book considers the importance of building home-school connections for science learning. Finally, chapter 5 reviews research and theory and discusses science content, methodology, and teaching strategies.

Next, chapters based upon content suggested by the Benchmarks for Science Literacy and the National Science Education Standards are presented. There are eight experiences based upon the content areas. These guides include sections for the teacher and for the children.

The section "For the Teacher" begins by identifying concepts key to learning science. Goals and objectives are stated. This section discusses concrete ideas for connecting children's home and family to the school, and describes how to evaluate and assess children's science learning.

The section "For the Children" consists of ideas for implementing the identified goals and objectives through thematic, integrated, and continual experiences. In this case, the guides are based on knowledge, skills, resources, and environments required for children to construct science concepts.

AUTHORS

Another important feature of the book is the expertise and background of the authors. Together, they bring a unique perspective to the book. Both have experienced Deweyan education. Both have worked in Head Start, childcare, and other early childhood settings and thus bring an intimate knowledge of practice to the text. And because both are researchers, the latest in theory and research in the field of early childhood education is represented in the text.

ACKNOWLEDGMENTS

We wish to thank Ann Davis, whose knowledge of active children and thoughtful guidance contributed to the development of this book. We appreciate the expertise of Sheryl Langner. Her careful attention to the details of book production merits special thanks. Thank you to Keli Gemrich for her assistance in getting the manuscript ready for production.

We would like to thank the following for their valuable suggestions and comments: Cecelia Benelli, Western Illinois University; Colin K. Ducolon, Champlain College; Deborah A. Moberly, Southeast Missouri State; and Colleen K. Randel, The University of Texas at Tyler.

About the Authors

Carol Seefeldt, Ph.D., is Professor Emeritus of human development at the Institute for Child Study, University of Maryland, College Park, where she taught graduate and undergraduate classes for 28 years. She received the Distinguished Scholar-Teacher Award from the university and has published 23 books and over 100 scholarly and research articles for teachers and parents. Her books include *Social Studies for the Preschool/Primary Child, Active Experiences for Active Children: Social Studies, Active Experiences for Active Children: Literacy Emerges,* and *Current Issues in Early Childhood Education* (the last three with Alice Galper), and *The Early Childhood Curriculum: Current Findings in Theory and Practice.*

During her 40 years in the field, Dr. Seefeldt has taught at every level from nursery school for 2-year-olds through the third grade. In Florida, she directed a church-related kindergarten, and served as Regional Training Officer for Project Head Start. She has conducted teacher-training programs in Japan and the Ukraine and has been a frequent guest on radio and television talk shows.

Alice Galper, Ph. D., educator and consultant, received her doctorate from the University of Maryland, College Park. Previously, she was a classroom teacher in New Hampshire and a Head Start Consultant in the Washington, DC, area. She was a professor of human development teaching graduate and undergraduate courses in early childhood and human development at Mt. Vernon College, Washington, DC, for nearly 20 years and at the University of Maryland. She assisted Carol Seefeldt on the research component of the Montgomery County Head Start—Public School Transition Demonstration. Currently she is on the adjunct faculty at the University of Maryland.

Alice's research has revolved around intergenerational attitudes and program evaluation. She has written many articles for such journals as *Child Development, Journal of Educational Psychology,* and *Early Childhood Research Quarterly.*

Alice presents workshops and papers regularly at the National Association for the Education of Young Children Conference, the Head Start Research Conference, and the Society for Research in Child Development Biennial Meetings, among others.

Active in community affairs, Alice has been appointed by Mayor Anthony Williams of Washington, DC, as cochair of the Interagency Coordinating Council of the DC Early Intervention Program for Infants and Toddlers, and she volunteers for Mary's Center for Maternal and Child Care, Inc.

Discover the Companion Website Accompanying This Book

THE PRENTICE HALL COMPANION WEBSITE: A VIRTUAL LEARNING ENVIRONMENT

Technology is a constantly growing and changing aspect of our field that is creating a need for content and resources. To address this emerging need, Prentice Hall has developed an online learning environment for students and professors alike—Companion Websites—to support our textbooks.

In creating a Companion Website, our goal is to build on and enhance what the textbook already offers. For this reason, the content for each user-friendly website is organized by topic and provides the professor and student with a variety of meaningful resources. Common features of a Companion Website include:

FOR THE PROFESSOR—

Every Companion Website integrates **Syllabus Manager™,** an online syllabus creation and management utility.

- **Syllabus Manager™** provides you, the instructor, with an easy, step-by-step process to create and revise syllabi, with direct links into Companion Website and other online content without having to learn HTML.

- Students may log on to your syllabus during any study session. All they need to know is the web address for the Companion Website and the password you've assigned to your syllabus.

- After you have created a syllabus using **Syllabus Manager™,** students may enter the syllabus for their course section from any point in the Companion Website.

- Clicking on a date, the student is shown the list of activities for the assignment. The activities for each assignment are linked directly to actual content, saving time for students.

- Adding assignments consists of clicking on the desired due date, then filling in the details of the assignment—name of the assignment, instructions, and whether or not it is a one-time or repeating assignment.

- In addition, links to other activities can be created easily. If the activity is online, a URL can be entered in the space provided, and it will be linked automatically in the final syllabus.

- Your completed syllabus is hosted on our servers, allowing convenient updates from any computer on the Internet. Changes you make to your syllabus are immediately available to your students at their next logon.

FOR THE STUDENT—

Topic Overviews—outline key concepts in topic areas

Web Links—general websites related to topic areas as well as associations and professional organizations

Read About It—timely articles that enable you to become more aware of important issues in early childhood education

Learn by Doing—put concepts into action, participate in activities, complete lesson plans, examine strategies, and more

For Teachers—access information that you will need to know as an in-service teacher, including information on materials, activities, lessons, curriculum, and state standards

Visit a School—visit a school's website to see concepts, theories, and strategies in action

Electronic Bluebook—send homework or essays directly to your instructor's email with this paperless form

Message Board—serves as a virtual bulletin board to post—or respond to—questions or comments to/from a national audience

Chat—real-time chat with anyone who is using the text anywhere in the country— ideal for discussion and study groups, class projects, etc.

To take advantage of these and other resources, please visit the *Active Experiences for Active Children: Science* Companion Website at

www.prenhall.com/seefeldt

Contents

————————————— PART ONE —————————————
Theory of Active Experiences   1

1 Experiences and Science in Early Childhood: Theory into Practice   3

Cognitive Theories: The Basis of Science Education for Young Children   5
How Concepts Build   6
Teaching Strategies for Science Learning   6
Summary   7

2 Active Children—Active Indoor Environments   9

The Essentials: Health, Safety, Inclusion, and Beauty   10
    Health and Safety, 10
    Planning for Inclusion, 11
    Beauty, 12
Indoor Spaces   12
    Integrating Spaces, 12
    Science Areas, 13
    Art Centers, 14
    Woodworking Center, 15
    Book and Library Centers, 15
    Sociodramatic Play Areas, 16
    Areas for Manipulatives, 17
    Block Areas, 17
    Water and Sand Areas, 17
    Music Areas, 17
    Computer Stations, 18
    Quiet Spaces, 18
The Teacher's Role   18
Summary   19

3 Active Children—Active Outdoor Environments   21

Why Plan for Outdoor Environments?   22
Space Planning   23

Science and Nature Discovery Areas, 23
Art Activities, 24
Math Activities, 24
Physical Activities, 25
Other Considerations, 25
The Teacher's Role   25
Summary   27

Building Connections to Home and Community Through Active Experiences   29

Out into the School   31
Inside the School Building, 32
Outside in the Natural Environment, 32
Out into the Neighborhood and Community   32
Basic Guidelines for Meaningful Field Experiences   33
Building Connections with the Neighborhood and Community   35
Natural Resources, 35
Visitors, 35
Zoos, 35
Science Centers and Museums, 36
The Home-School Connection   36
Summary   38

Experiences and Science Content   39

Knowledge of Children   40
Knowledge of the Subject Matter—Science   41
Organizing Children's Experiences   42
Bringing Knowledge of Children and Content Together   43
Expanding and Extending Firsthand Experiences   44
Summary   45

PART TWO
Guides to Active Experiences   47

Living Things Grow and Change: Seeds and Plants   49

For the Teacher   50
What You'll Need to Know, 50
Key Concepts, 50
Goals and Objectives, 50

What You'll Need, 50
The Home-School Connection, 52
Evaluating and Assessing Children's Learning, 52
For the Children   53
Using Process Skills with Seeds, 53
Using Process Skills with Seeds and Plants, 53
Using Children's Books to Motivate Active Experiences with Seeds and Plants, 54
Using Arts and Crafts to Document Active Experiences with Seeds and Plants, 55
Reflecting, 55
Extending and Expanding to the Early Primary Grades, 55
Documenting Children's Learning, 57

Living Things Grow and Change: Insects and Small Animals   65

For the Teacher   66
What You'll Need to Know, 66
Key Concepts, 66
Goals and Objectives, 66
What You'll Need, 67
The Home-School Connection, 68
Evaluating and Assessing Children's Learning, 69
For the Children   69
Observing Small Animals: Insects, 69
Environments and Life Cycles, 70
Nests, 70
*Recognizing Children's Books in Which Animals Are Depicted with Human
    Attributes and Feelings, 71*
Classroom Pets or Not, 71
Reflecting, 72
Extending and Expanding to the Early Primary Grades, 72
Documenting Children's Learning, 73

I Am a Scientist   79

For the Teacher   80
What You'll Need to Know, 80
Key Concepts, 80
Goals and Objectives, 80
What You'll Need, 80
The Home-School Connection, 81
Evaluating and Assessing Children's Learning, 82
For the Children   82
Learning to Observe, 82
Learning to Question, 83
Planning and Conducting Investigations, 84
Documenting Children's Learning, 85

How Toys Work   87

For the Teacher   88
   What You'll Need to Know, 88
   Key Concepts, 88
   Goals and Objectives, 88
   What You'll Need, 88
   The Home-School Connection, 89
   Evaluating and Assessing Children's Learning, 89
For the Children   89
   Sources of Energy, 89
   Vibrations, 92
   Documenting Children's Learning, 92

 The Earth: Water   95

For the Teacher   96
   What You'll Need to Know, 96
   Key Concepts, 96
   Goals and Objectives, 96
   What You'll Need, 97
   The Home-School Connection, 98
   Evaluating and Assessing Children's Learning, 99
For the Children   99
   Indoor and Outdoor Activities, 99
   Reflecting, 101
   Extending and Expanding to the Early Primary Grades, 101
   Documenting Children's Learning, 102

 The Earth: Rocks and Minerals   107

For the Teacher   108
   What You'll Need to Know, 108
   Key Concepts, 108
   Goals and Objectives, 108
   What You'll Need, 109
   The Home-School Connection, 110
   Evaluating and Assessing Children's Learning, 111
For the Children   111
   Indoor and Outdoor Activities, 111
   Reflecting, 113
   Extending and Expanding to the Early Primary Grades, 113
   Documenting Children's Learning, 114

7 **The Human Body: The Senses** **119**

For the Teacher   120
   What You'll Need to Know, 120
   Key Concepts, 120
   Goals and Objectives, 120
   What You'll Need, 120
   The Home-School Connection, 122
   Evaluating and Assessing Children's Learning, 122

For the Children   123
   Sound, 123
   Smell, 124
   Touch, 125
   Taste, 126
   Sight, 126
   Reflecting, 127
   Extending and Expanding to the Early Primary Grades, 127
   Documenting Children's Learning, 128

 8 **Healthy Bodies** **133**

For the Teacher   134
   What You'll Need to Know, 134
   Key Concepts, 134
   Goals and Objectives, 134
   What You'll Need, 135
   The Home-School Connection, 136
   Evaluating and Assessing Children's Learning, 138

For the Children   138
   Indoor and Outdoor Activities, 138
   Reflecting, 140
   Extending and Expanding to the Early Primary Grades, 140
   Documenting Children's Learning, 141

References   **145**

Resources   **148**

Index   **151**

PART ONE

Theory of Active Experiences

Experiences and Science in Early Childhood
Theory into Practice

All genuine education comes about through experience . . . but not all experiences are genuinely or equally educative.

John Dewey, 1938, p. 13

Active Experiences for Active Children—Science guides teachers of 3- to 5-year-old children in planning and implementing meaningful learning experiences and skills in the sciences for children in childcare settings, nursery schools, Head Start, and kindergartens. Some themes are extended and expanded with ideas for children in the early primary grades. The book is based on the premise that activities are simply that—isolated, one-shot occurrences. They begin and end quickly. They give children something to do but not something to learn.

Experiences continue. They may last a couple of hours or a day, but usually they continue over weeks, even months, as in the Project Approach (Helm and Katz, 2001). Unlike isolated activities that are fleeting, experiences are filled with integrated learning. This book provides in-depth science experiences for young children based on the very latest research and publications in the field of science education.

In the last 10 years, several important documents have been written by science educators that are consistent with the guidelines for science proposed by the National Association for the Education of Young Children: *Science for All Americans,* 1989; *Benchmarks for Science Literacy,* 1993; *National Science Education Standards,* 1996; and *NSTA Pathways to the Science Standards: Elementary School Edition,* 1997. In addition, several conferences were held to join leaders in science education with early childhood experts, including the Forum on Early Childhood Science, Mathematics, and Technology Education (1998). Several strong themes emerged from the efforts:

• The introduction of children to the essential experiences of science inquiry and explorations must begin at an early age.

• The child's prior knowledge should be assessed before teachers provide new experiences.

• Preschool-level and primary-level science is an active enterprise. Rather than the memorization of facts, young children should be engaged in hands-on, inquiry learning. The emphasis should be on gaining experience with natural and social phenomena and on enjoying their explorations. Fundamental concepts and skills develop as children have the chance to ask questions, conduct investigations, collect data, and apply their problem-solving skills to new situations.

• There must be an emphasis on group as well as individual teaching approaches. Much of science learning is a cooperative endeavor.

The documents importantly emphasize content standards in each area of the science curriculum. The content standards are arranged by age. For example, The Benchmarks suggest that in the content area Living Environment (Cells), by the end of the second grade, children should know that

- magnifiers help people see things they could not see without them

- most living things need water, food, and air

The content suggested by these documents and the experiences that follow in this book have integrity and meaning. For example, what content are children learning when they are asked to make a cherry tree by pasting cotton balls a teacher has painstakingly tinted pink on a tree trunk drawn on a large sheet of brown paper by the teacher? Are children learning that cotton balls are cherry blossoms?

What content could children learn about cherry trees? Meaningful content might include the concepts that trees bud, bloom, and produce fruit in season. By observing cherry trees throughout the year, making and recording predictions of when they will bloom, what color the blossoms will be, and what will happen when they fall, children actually experience cherry blossoms and trees. Unlike learning about cherry trees by being told pink cotton balls are cherry blossoms, children are being introduced to concepts about trees that are real, meaningful, and have integrity.

This book, *Active Experiences for Active Children—Science,* makes clear connections between the active theme-based science experiences suggested in later chapters and the benchmarks and content standards. (See chapter 4 for the organizational scheme.)

COGNITIVE THEORIES: THE BASIS OF SCIENCE EDUCATION FOR YOUNG CHILDREN

The role of active experiences in learning was identified by John Dewey and Maria Montessori in the early 20th century. While modified by later researchers, the theories of John Dewey continue to be highly regarded by a large number of early childhood professionals for their emphasis on first-hand learning in the here-and-now world, child-initiated learning, and age-appropriate learning experiences and content.

Jean Piaget (1973), through his clinical interviews, researched the position that knowledge is constructed in the mind of the learner. He believed that young children think differently, in most circumstances, than do older children and adults. Thus, young children require a special kind of curriculum because their thinking is more concrete and less logical. For example, according to Piaget (1973), children in the Preoperational Stage (which encompasses the age group covered by this book) focus on one variable at a time, such as length or width, and are egocentric and animistic. That is, they believe that the world revolves around them, have trouble taking the point of view of another, and impute life to inanimate things. More recently, other theorists have argued that the reason young children think differently is their very lack of experience with the world. The Benchmarks and Content Standards do take a developmental view of science teaching, cautioning teachers, for example, not to reinforce young children's beliefs that animals have thoughts and feelings similar to their own.

As discussed later in chapter 4, Lev Vygotsky (1986) added significantly to Piaget's theories by postulating that the important factors in moving children to higher levels of thought are the significant and more accomplished others around them. Thus, if an adult believes that the child is very close to constructing a concept, he may act to ask a question, provide a tool, or suggest a course of action that will move the child forward. Good questions motivate children. When students are asked open-ended questions, they will pose innovative questions of their own, thus expanding their capacity for creative thinking and problem solving.

As a result of the synthesis of the previously mentioned theoretical positions and new thinking on children's acquisition of knowledge, the dominant theory upon which science teaching today is based is *constructivism,* the belief that children build knowledge (concepts) internally by interacting with their world to construct meaning. "As the Standards point out, students have to construct, or build, their *own* knowledge in a process that is individual and social. Students have to take an active role in their own learning. This teaching/learning relationship is called constructivism" (Lowery, 1997, p. 7). Because children acquire knowledge at different paces and through different learning styles, it is also important for teachers to provide instruction that meets the individual needs of young children.

HOW CONCEPTS BUILD

Science concepts grow and develop in infancy. Current research on brain development emphasizes the importance of early stimulation in developing brain connections from birth. While this book is not structured to provide experiences for infants, caregivers should understand that infants explore the world with their senses and should provide many opportunities for them to do so. If babies do not have things to look at, touch, smell, and hear, they will be deprived of the structures through which further knowledge is acquired. Toddlers need to be free to safely discover things on their own. They need things to grasp, carry, sort, push, and pull. Through the daily schedule they will also begin to develop a sense of time.

Although their primary avenue for concept learning is exploration, preschool- and kindergarten-aged children (sometimes with the help of an adult) can

- observe
- count
- organize
- record, document, and reflect

As they begin to collect and organize data to answer a question, new concepts and skills emerge.

TEACHING STRATEGIES FOR SCIENCE LEARNING

The National Science Education Standards (1996) describe what teachers of all grade levels should know and be able to do. They include the following:

• Planning inquiry-based science programs. Encourage students to observe, collect, handle, describe, become puzzled by, and ask questions about.

• Guiding and facilitating student learning. Engage students actively. Provide them with many and varied opportunities for collecting, sorting, and cataloging, using science instruments appropriate to their level, and systematically observing.

• Engaging in ongoing assessment of teaching and student learning. The types of assessment suggested are performance based, portfolios, open-ended questions, and science journal writing.

- Developing environments that enable students to learn science.

- Creating communities of science learners who debate and discuss their findings. Design projects that require collaborative participation, and provide many opportunities for written and oral expression.

Additionally, considerations of equity are critical in the science teaching standards. Teachers will want to model acceptance and tolerance and support individual learning styles. All students are capable of full participation in the science program, and efforts should be made to assist children who are nonnative speakers and compensate for children's inadequate experiential backgrounds.

The teacher must not only be an active participant in finding out the answers to science problems, but may use several teaching strategies to facilitate the development of science concepts. The following are essential to planning and participating in effective science learnings:

- The provision of an interesting and rich environment for the children. Here the teacher serves as facilitator, observes the children's spontaneous activity, notes progress, and encourages the children in their explorations.

- The initiation of informal learning experiences as a child is engaged in naturalistic exploration. These experiences are usually not preplanned, but arise when the teacher senses that a child is on the right track, but needs some additional cues to solve a problem. This strategy further involves taking advantage of the "teachable moment" to reinforce children's discoveries.

- The planning of structured experiences for both small and large groups around the major content areas identified in the Benchmarks and the Science Education Standards. The teacher will want to identify major themes such as the Earth: Water, or the Earth: Rocks and Minerals; gather resources for both adults and children; and plan experiences and experiments through which children can answer their questions about their earth.

- The modeling of effective problem-solving techniques. Teachers are powerful models for children. If they are enthusiastic and open about science teaching, children will adopt similar attitudes.

Each of these strategies is developmentally appropriate. They should all be used at one time or another as part of an effective science program. Additionally, children need plenty of time to engage in the process of science learning and to reflect on their findings.

SUMMARY

Children learn from content-based science experiences because they are involved with their hands and their minds, and are actively engaged in making sense of themselves in their world. Because experiences are embedded in children's here-and-now world, they are of interest to children. The Benchmarks suggest that teachers start with questions about phenomena that are interesting and familiar to students, such as nature. This interest motivates young children to meet the challenges of a science program and become successful learners.

Theme-based experiences continue. When children leave school for the day, they will know there will be something for them to continue doing when they return the next day. The fact that the experiences in this book are based on concepts key to the discipline not only gives them intellectual integrity, but offers children continuity of content. And because the experiences are connected to the child's family and community, there is a continuous thread of learning in children's lives. The Benchmarks, Science Education Standards, and this book emphasize the vital roles of families and communities in facilitating and enhancing science education in and out of the classroom. Many resources are suggested in the chapters that follow.

Finally, this is an excellent time to be writing about science experiences for young children. The evidence and support are now present for early childhood educators to propose a science program that requires different content and strategies from those previously based upon memorization and rote learning.

2

Active Children—Active Indoor Environments

Although sciencing can occur spontaneously, what children gain can be enhanced and increased by planning. Both the classroom environment and our teaching strategies should encourage active sciencing.

Kilmer & Hoffman, 1995, p. 58

Centers of learning are ideally suited for the social interaction essential to the child's construction of meaning. Rich and challenging classroom talk between children and adult-child dialogue foster peer-based learning and assistance from more competent adults to reach higher conceptual levels. The range of skills that can be achieved with adult guidance and peer collaboration far exceeds what a child can learn alone or in whole class instruction. This chapter presents general guidelines for designing environments for children—health and safety, inclusion, and beauty. More emphasis is placed on science centers, but the whole environment is considered as a laboratory for learning.

If active children are to learn through active experiences, then their environment must be carefully, thoughtfully, and deliberately arranged. Indoor spaces should be structured so children can

- engage in meaningful firsthand learning, taking the initiative for their learning, and making choices and decisions;

- work, play, and interact freely with others, both peers and adults;

- use language, talking, listening, writing, and reading in connection with their interactions with their physical world and socially with others;

- experience success as they gain new skills through interaction with their physical environment; and

- be alone so they can reflect on their experiences.

Beginning with the essentials—health, safety, inclusion, and beauty—teachers plan for children's meaningful learning experiences by deliberately arranging the indoor learning environment. Teachers not only deliberately arrange physical environments for active learning, but they also plan ways of interacting with children that foster and promote children's learning and development.

THE ESSENTIALS: HEALTH, SAFETY, INCLUSION, AND BEAUTY

Health and Safety

Specific health and safety concerns are delineated for each of the activities in the chapters to come. The following are more general concerns. The indoor environment must be set up with each child's health and safety in mind:

- Equipment is checked for sharp edges, loose pieces that could cause accidents, or small parts that children might swallow or stuff in their ears.

- Most materials provided for the children are unbreakable, although in some instances, such as making an aquarium, glass is the best good choice, and adult guidance is essential.

- Equipment is disinfected by daily washing with detergent in water, rinsing with clear water, wiping or spraying with a solution of two tablespoons of chlorine bleach and one gallon of water, and sun or air drying.

- Use of all heat sources is well supervised, and outlets are covered when not in use.

- Tubs and pools of water are closely supervised.

- Tools such as knives and hammers are in good condition, and their use is carefully observed.

Safety is a fundamental concern in the science curriculum. Teachers must know and apply the necessary safety regulations in the storage, use, and care of the materials used by students. Locked cabinets are a must when materials are not in use. In addition, careful rules must be established for the care of fish and small animals if they reside in the classroom. Parents should be contacted about any allergies that would prevent their child from participating in a particular science project.

Space will also be provided for active experiences for children that foster healthy physical and psychological development. Both the National Science Education Standards and Benchmarks for Science Literacy suggest that students become acquainted with factors that foster healthy bodies and develop an understanding of pleasant and unpleasant feelings.

Planning for Inclusion

The physical environment can be arranged in ways that enable all children to participate to the fullest extent possible in all experiences. To permit use of a wheelchair, remove physical barriers, provide wider paths, and arrange work spaces and activity units to offer shelter from intrusion or interference (Louglin & Suina, 1982). More accomplished peers may model and teach the use of materials in the science center. When safety is an issue, a "buddy" may be assigned to a child who is less able. Children with special needs may profit from a multisensory approach to the teaching of science.

Reducing the amount of visual stimulation in a given area aids children who are visually impaired. Teachers have found that they can add textures or raised patterns to the walls to enable visually impaired children to locate themselves in space. Tactile experiences are also valuable for nonimpaired peers since they foster learning through touch. Others find small shelving units, with a few materials on each shelf, as helpful.

Hearing-impaired children require more visual stimulation and less auditory distraction. Felt pads on tabletops, carpeted shelves and other work surfaces, as well as the clear display of all materials and equipment will be helpful (Seefeldt & Barbour, 1998). Teachers may actively foster children's understanding and appreciation of the senses and sensory impairments through active experiences with the five senses. (Specific activities are discussed in experience 7.)

Louglin and Suina (1982) do not believe that teachers need to reduce the amount and variety of learning materials within a classroom to accommodate the needs of children with physical disabilities: "Rather than reducing the amount and variety of learning materials, or simplifying their level to meet children's handicaps, the host teachers removed barriers for children with special needs by increasing the variation of materials, which also expanded learning possibilities for all children" (p. 211). Mallory (1998) suggests that small groups of two to four learners provide an optimal structure for fostering cognitive development and social participation in inclusive classrooms: "Given the heterogeneity that exists in inclusive classrooms, it is logical to assume that whole group activity is not likely to be an effective means for assuring that the particular needs of individual learners will be met" (p. 228).

Beauty

Aesthetics and beauty must be considered for young children growing up in a world that increasingly prefers highways and large housing developments to green space and historic buildings. Aesthetics means being sensitive to beauty in the environment—in nature and art. "Such sensitivity is fostered not by talking about beauty but by experiencing it in a variety of forms" (Wilson, 1995, p. 4). It is important to note that beauty resides not only in the natural environment, but also in vibrant city neighborhoods and small historic towns.

The childcare centers in Reggio Emilia, Italy, illustrate the wonder and beauty of environments created with aesthetics in mind. Stepping into a childcare center in Reggio, one knows immediately that the environment has been carefully arranged to simplify and order the children's world as well as surround them with beauty (Seefeldt, 1995).

Open rooms, filled with light and air, are simply and elegantly arranged. This clear, clean conceptualization of an environment is especially appropriate for active children who learn through active experiences, and facilitates the child's construction of beginning science concepts. Integrating conceptual learning in various subject matter areas with artistic expression, children are encouraged to make visual or symbolic representations of their activities in a variety of media.

Everywhere you look there is something beautiful to wonder over and ponder. Mirrors of all types are found throughout the center. Bits of mirrors and colored glass hang in front of windows to catch a sunbeam and bounce it back to children. Long horizontal mirrors are mounted near the floor so children can watch themselves as they build with blocks or play with others.

Plants and flowers are ever present throughout the center in classrooms, in lunchrooms and sleeping rooms, and in the bathrooms. Children's artwork is mounted, framed, and displayed, serving not only to stimulate children to thought and permit them to document and reflect on past experiences, but also to inform others of the experiences children are having in and out of the center. The home is intimately connected with the centers.

This emphasis on aesthetics in Reggio "reflects an appreciation of detail and sensitivity to design consistent with Italian cultural tradition of creative endeavors" (Mallory & New, 1994, p. 10). Nevertheless, children everywhere, not just in Italy, deserve to live and learn in environments that are aesthetically pleasing and visually appealing (Seefeldt & Barbour, 1998). Bredekamp (1993) reflects "that perhaps we, in America, have set our sights too low in our vision of excellence" (p. 13). Too often in programs for young children little attention is given to the beauty of the classroom. Commercial posters and decorations take the place of objects of beauty and child-inspired art.

INDOOR SPACES

Integrating Spaces

Organizing indoor spaces with centers of interest permits active children to engage in active experiences. Centers of interest are areas of the room that are clearly defined with either actual dividers or suggested boundaries. They contain materials and equipment organized to promote specific types of learning. The materials are carefully arranged so children can see the choices available and make decisions about which materials they will use and how they will use them (Bronson, 1995).

Yet, while areas are defined, teachers should work toward an integrated curriculum framework so that science, for example, becomes a part of the social studies, arts and crafts, music and movement, mathematics, and emergent literacy (for younger children) and the language arts (for older children). "When we integrate science experiences with other curriculum areas, we help children enhance their mental performance. As we enrich the range of connections and relationships among different styles of absorbing, associating, and applying information, children form more intricate neural pathways in their brains, and concept retention increases" (Harlan & Rivkin, 2000, p. 11). The integrated curriculum will be emphasized in the chapters that follow.

Children's literature, for example, is an excellent way to integrate science throughout the early childhood curriculum. An important part of an effective science curriculum is a classroom library with a wide variety of science-related children's literature, both fiction and nonfiction. Teachers may read books such as *Everybody Needs a Rock,* by B. Baylor, to stimulate children's interest in rocks and minerals. Stories, guides, and reference books should also be placed in the various centers of interest for inquiry and stimulation. As part of a theme on pets, children can

- read about various pets of fact and fiction.
- find out what various pets eat, their preferred habitat, and how to care for them.
- chart the habits of classroom pets (when they eat, sleep, play).
- write about pets using science journals, posters, poetry, and stories.
- create movement activities, finger plays, and drama based on pets.
- depict pets using many art forms.
- develop a caring and sensitive attitude toward pets.

In addition, if pets are kept in the classroom, children can make and record rules for their care and handling.

Science Areas

The National Science Education Standards suggest that "teachers of science design and manage learning environments that provide students with the time, space, and resources needed for learning science" (National Research Council, 1996, p. 11). They plan the use of this space to allow students to work safely in groups of various sizes at various tasks, to maintain their work in progress, and to display their results. Wonderful displays of the results of children's inquiry are often ignored in early childhood classrooms. They provide an opportunity for children to reflect upon their work and validate the importance of their efforts. Teachers also provide students with the opportunity to contribute their ideas about use of space and furnishings (National Research Council, 1996).

Spaces are needed where children can actively experiment with and explore the life, health, and physical sciences. Natural science and earth and space science experiences may be best reserved for the outdoor environment, although there are many opportunities to construct experiments and displays indoors. The center or centers should provide opportunities for children to observe, classify, compare, measure, communicate, experiment, make predictions, and reach conclusions. The teacher will want to provide materials that will excite the child's natural interest, pose many questions, and promote active inquiry.

One teacher arranged a pitcher of water and small cups on a table next to small containers of instant coffee, tea leaves, dirt, sand, beans, sugar, and salt. She posed a question for the children: "Which things will dissolve in water and which ones will not?" A clipboard with a checklist for children to record their findings was placed beside the center. Children were encouraged to discuss and negotiate their conclusions. The children later presented the center as part of a series of experiments for their families to try at the conclusion of a science unit.

Other science learning centers could be equipped with things to weigh, measure, and balance. Magnets, compasses, prisms, magnifying glasses, and different kinds of mirrors and colored cellophane also promote children's active explorations.

Machines to take apart—clocks, pencil sharpeners, instrument-panel boards (all of which have been safety proofed)—along with screwdrivers and wrenches fascinate children, who are curious about how things work. One group of 5-year-olds worked for days taking apart an alarm clock and recorded each step in detailed drawings that the teacher displayed to document the process and then stored for later reflection.

Living things may be a part of the science area if they are well cared for and are not safety hazards for children. It is a desirable goal for children to learn about the life cycle, yet too many premature deaths of classroom animals result from poor care and a lack of safety rules in early childhood classrooms. Plants and insects are often a better alternative. An ant farm, created from a discarded large food jar, intrigues children, as does a butterfly farm or a worm garden. Sometimes teachers will want to invite a pet to visit the classroom. Children should consult books and formulate questions about the pet before the visit. Answers should be recorded in science journals or on chart paper.

Whatever active experiences spring from the children's interests or are planned by teachers, it is important that enough time is available for extended investigations. Teachers make time for students to work in varied groupings—alone, in pairs, in small groups, as a whole class—and on varied tasks, such as reading, conducting experiments, reflecting, writing, and discussing. Beginning to build scientific understanding in children takes time on a daily basis and over the school year.

Art Centers

Through the visual arts, children are able to give expression to their ideas, imaginations, feelings, and emotions. This expression is necessary if children are to reflect on their experiences. Each day, children should have a choice of whether to draw, paint, model, cut and paste, or construct something. Materials are arranged on tables or shelves that are easily accessible to children. Easels, a variety of brushes, and fresh, thick paints are available every day. At other times, areas of the floor, or a table or two, can also be used for painting. All types of drawing materials—crayons, markers, chalk, even pencils for 5-year-olds—are stored on open shelves for children's selection (Dighe, Calomiris, & Van Zutphen, 1998). A junk box, with every type of material imaginable and a sewing box for 5-year-olds, equipped with threads, bits of fabric, buttons, and large blunt needles, are available. There is a separate area for clay and modeling materials.

Because the visual arts give children a way to organize, reflect upon, and present their ideas or emotions, art materials are chosen that enable children to do so. For example, a group of children took a walking trip to the park to see the cherry trees blooming near their center. When they returned, they found the art center equipped with a variety of pink, lavender, and white paints and papers.

Manipulating modeling clay and observing its properties, painting with tempera paints and observing drips and how colors mix, and organizing and sorting materials for a collage help children to understand science concepts and integrate them with other subject matter areas.

Woodworking Center

A center for woodworking gives children other opportunities to re-create their experiences. Woodworking involves such a variety of skills, tools, and materials that there are endless opportunities for using the processes of science such as classification, comparisons, measurement, and predictions about how the finished construction will look. Through trial and error, children will also draw conclusions such as "long, fat nails will split soft wood." Children are endlessly fascinated by woodworking, but teachers must closely supervise and co-construct learnings with the children.

A place for children to construct three-dimensional objects should also be included. Children can use any material with which to work. In Reggio, found objects—boxes, feathers, shells, sequins, paper, silk and brocade scraps—are stored on open shelves in aesthetically pleasing ways, inviting children to choose what materials they will use and how they will arrange them. The design and creation of three-dimensional objects help children to master science concepts that revolve around weight and balance.

Book and Library Centers

The library area is a place where books are arranged along with tables, chairs, soft carpet, and cushions enticing children to stay and read. It is a place located away from other distractions where children will find every type of book—poetry, stories, folktales, picture books, reference books and materials, biography, historical fiction, and books composed of photographs—sections from the newspaper specifically geared to children's work, and children's newspapers and magazines.

All children should find themselves reflected in these books. Books depicting the lives of children with special needs, as well as children of diverse cultural, racial, and ethnic backgrounds, will be selected (Blaska & Lynch, 1998).

Catalogues are fun to include. Children can use these as "wish books" or to compare, contrast, or classify the contents. If two or more of the same catalog are in the area, children will play games with them: "I'm looking at a toy. It's red and black, and children ride on it. Can you find it?"

Mounted pictures cut from magazines and depicting a topic the children are studying are excellent for younger children to sort through and carry around with them. Books dictated or written by the children, or photo albums and stories written by the teacher, are other favorites. Some library areas also include flannel boards with cut-out figures for children to put into sequence or to use to retell a story by themselves or with a group of children.

Some books may be organized as a take-home library for the children so their learning experiences can continue when they are home. Linking science with literature is a natural way for parents to extend and support science in the home. A simple check-out sheet with two markers attached can be mounted above the books. The children can place a check with the red marker when they take out a book and a check with the black marker when they return it. Books will also be displayed around the room. In one Head Start center, children observed a construction site and were fascinated with the trucks, cranes, and earthmoving equipment they saw. When they returned to the room, the teacher placed several books on trucks and construction vehicles in an open box next to the blocks. Children began consulting these as they created their own buildings.

Although both nonfiction and fiction books can be used to support the development of science concepts, it is important that the information is accurate. The books should further spur children to investigate something or engage in hands-on science experiences.

Sociodramatic Play Areas

The primary sociodramatic play area is the housekeeping center, where children engage in playing house with others, enacting the roles they observe in their homes. From time to time, other sociodramatic play areas will be arranged so children can play store, gas station, office, or post office, or act out some other theme. All of these areas support the science curriculum as science concepts are integrated into play themes.

Children of all ages find the housekeeping area continually appealing. This is the place where dramatic play flourishes, and here children find a way to link their home to their school. Children are free, when playing house, to feel big and in control when they take on the role of a parent, or weak and helpless when they play as if they were a baby.

Props reflecting children's home life are found in the housekeeping area. Some may reflect their parents' work world—briefcases, hard hats, work boots, or tools representative of parents' work. Others, such as dishes, pots and pans, baby dolls representing all ethnic groups, cribs, baby bottles, full-length and hand mirrors, alarm clocks, microwaves, discarded cell phones, calculators, computers, and clothes of all types, will reflect children's life at home.

Materials will be selected that encourage children to use written as well as spoken language, including notepads, calendars, discarded checkbooks, address books, and pencils, markers, and pens for children to write with as they indulge in dramatic play. Reading materials such as newspapers, magazines, phone books, and fiction and informational books enhance play.

No two housekeeping centers will be exactly alike or equipped with the same materials because each center will contain props representing the culture and activities of the children's homes. In one kindergarten class, a diverse group of children were having a heated discussion in the housekeeping kitchen about the name of a dumpling. The teacher saw this as an opportunity to teach children how foods such as dumplings are made by families all over the world, but have slightly different ingredients and different names. Through stories and cooking activities the children explored ravioli, wontons, pierogies, and samosas.

Other areas for sociodramatic play are appropriate. When children visit their parents who work in offices, or visit the school's office, an area for office play is applicable. A table framed with cardboard walls becomes an office cubicle. Telephone receipt books, bookkeeping forms—anything that looks official and has space for writing—along with pencils, erasers, and markers of all kinds belong in the office. Children enjoy exploring staplers, pencil sharpeners, and others office tools, especially rubber stamps with stamp pads.

Based on children's experiences with their world, other dramatic play areas will be pertinent. For instance, if children have visited

- a post office, then a post office with envelopes, stamps, machines to weigh objects, and cubbyholes in which to sort mail would be created.

- a fast-food restaurant, then a restaurant with aprons, hats, trays, boxes for food, cups and bottles, a cash register, and pretend money would be added.

- a supermarket, then a store, complete with a cash register, money, all types of food containers, cans, boxes, bags to pack, old cash register receipts, and other materials, would be arranged so children could reenact their visit to the supermarket, taking turns being shoppers, clerks, bakers, or shelf stockers.

- a doctor's office, then an office complete with a waiting room, charts of the body, stethoscopes, unbreakable thermometers, tools to test the reflexes, and white coats can be added. Bandages are a must to treat pretend patients or dolls in need of aid. Small cots may provide a temporary resting place. Writing pads and pencils should be available for dispensing prescriptions.

Areas for Manipulatives

In manipulative centers, children learn a good deal about the physical sciences. Teachers arrange age-appropriate puzzles, board games, matching and bingo games, pegs and pegboards, construction sets, small plastic or wooden blocks or tiles, Tinkertoys, erector sets, large Legos, and other materials. All these give children needed practice in observing, ordering, discriminating, classifying, and predicting.

A few sets of regular decks of cards and materials such as large beads and buttons, nuts and bolts, washers, seashells, and other objects are important additions for sorting, counting, and categorizing. Things for children to string—beads, bottle caps with holes in them, and shoestrings—are enjoyable. Using pull toys with removable wheels to discover the difference between moving toys with wheels and without them, and inventing machines using Tinkertoys and other building sets with gears, levers, or pulleys give children the active experiences they need to build science concepts.

Block Areas

Blocks and spaces in which to build are essential. Ideally, blocks should be stored on open shelves with a place for each type of block. Storing all rectangular blocks on the same shelf, for example, fosters children's ability to classify. A complete set of wooden unit blocks is the best investment a center or program can make. If these are unaffordable, blocks can be made out of paper cartons. Science concepts are fostered as children observe, build, measure, compare, predict, begin to learn about spatial relations, and construct building plans.

Water and Sand Areas

Children need indoor areas where they can explore the properties of both water and sand and develop concepts of the surfaces of the world in which they live. Water is easy to provide. All that is needed is a low table; a small, plastic pan; some plastic cups and containers—spoons, funnels, plastic tubing, straws; and a small amount of water. Children build science concepts through active experiences in using containers, watching water flow, making bubbles in water, and observing how water is absorbed by paper towels.

Sand, in a sand table, a plastic tub, or an old wading pool, can readily be available indoors. As with water play, children learn beginning concepts through the use of a variety of containers from which to pour and measure sand, or mold and shape sand into various forms. Water should be handy if children are to build with sand, however.

Music Areas

A quiet part of the room, away from other activities, can be established as the music center—a space in which to listen to, as well as make, music. Here, children listen to a tape, operating a CD player by themselves. Or they play with whatever musical instruments can be on hand. Science concepts abound as children begin to understand sound and vibration, as well as enjoy various musical instruments. Environmental cassette tapes and CDs may be added to correspond to current science topics such as the ocean.

Computer Stations

Several computers can be set up with age-appropriate programs that

- teach some skills more effectively than traditional and less expensive methods and materials.

- have the potential to help children develop higher-order thought skills like judging, evaluating, analyzing, or synthesizing information (Wright & Shade, 1994).

- present accurate information.

- do not emphasize war, violence, or discrimination against women or any racial/ethnic group.

- provide for more than one child to work with a program.

- teach a concept or concepts that children are unable to obtain through an active experience or inquiry.

Quiet Spaces

Children need space to be alone with one or two others. It may be a corner of the room with a few pillows on the floor, a small nook in the library area, or a chair and table somewhere away from the other centers. Every room needs a space—wherever it is, or whatever it consists of—where children can be away from the group, relax, calm themselves, and think.

THE TEACHER'S ROLE

Without a concerned, interested, and knowledgeable adult, even the best equipped indoor spaces fall short of offering children meaningful experiences. Based on knowledge of children, of their experiences at home and in the community, it is the adult who

- selects, arranges, and changes the indoor centers, making sure the spaces remain uncluttered, safe, inviting, and accessible to all children.

- schedules large blocks of time during the morning and afternoon for active experiences.

- provides a background of meaningful experiences with people, places, and things so children will have ideas—including the imaginary, feelings, and emotions to express through play.

Most of all, however, it is the teacher who interacts with children in ways that clarify, extend, and expand their knowledge and skills.

- Teachers observe and supervise children as they play. Observations can focus on the total group of children or on individuals. The progress children are making, the skills they are gaining, and the things they still need to learn can be noted. When needed, teachers step in—setting limits, clarifying rules, removing broken toys or objects, and supporting children in their attempts to learn new concepts, skills, and attitudes.

- Teachers enter into joint activities with children, working collaboratively with them on a problem or task, such as comparing seeds from four different familiar plants.

- Teachers extend children's play by entering into the play scene. A teacher of 3-year-olds subtly encouraged children who were playing food store by saying things like, "Where can I pay for my bananas?" and "This would be a good place to arrange the cereal." These suggestions led children to organize and extend their play.

- Teachers use language to promote children's learning, naming things in the children's environment and giving information when needed: "That sign says, 'STOP.' When we see it, we stop and look both ways before crossing the street."

- Teachers ask a variety of questions that lead children to new learning: "Let's count the acorns; how many do you have?" "How are they alike/different?" "How are you going to mix the colors for your painting?" "Is your suitcase light or heavy?"

- Teachers offer assistance to help a child solve a problem or achieve the next level of functioning: "Here, I'll hold this piece of wood while you attach that part."

- Teachers plan and help children select activities that are appropriate for individual children's development and background of experiences.

- Teachers set expectations for classroom behaviors that are consistent with children's emerging cognitive and social capabilities (Berk & Winsler, 1995).

- Teachers demonstrate how to do something, supporting children as they try.

- Teachers give specific directions and information.

- Teachers seriously enter into conversations about children's work, focusing on the children, their work, and their ideas. Lilian Katz (1993) observed that teachers often seem reluctant to engage children in meaningful conversations and focus more on giving positive feedback rather than talking about content, relationships, or even what the child is doing.

- Teachers carefully structure their interactions with children to move them forward in concept development through understanding of what Vygotsky (1978) termed the *zone of proximal development.*

- Teachers ensure that all children are able to take part in centers of interest.

SUMMARY

Active children need indoor spaces that are specifically designed to foster active experiences with the sciences. Planning indoor environments begins with making certain the spaces are healthy, safe, beautiful, and accessible to children with special needs.

Indoor spaces are arranged with centers of interests, but science is integrated throughout. Centers organize children's environment, let them see the choices available to them, and give them the means to work and play cooperatively with others.

As Dewey (1938) suggested, the role of the teacher is more complex and more intimate when children are actively engaged in experiential learning. Teachers schedule large blocks of time for children's indoor experiences, and actively teach, guide, focus, and interact with children.

3

Active Children—Active Outdoor Environments

Students should be actively involved in exploring phenomena that interest them both in and out of class. These investigations should be fun and exciting, opening the door to even more things to explore.

American Association for the Advancement of Science, 1993, p. 6

WHY PLAN FOR OUTDOOR ENVIRONMENTS?

Children need the challenge and freedom inherent in outdoor play. Through rough-and-tumble outdoor play, children have the opportunity to develop feelings of confidence not only in themselves and their bodies, but also in others and in their natural environment. Children with physical disabilities find outdoor play of special value. Here they can strengthen large muscles. Depending on their needs, they can walk up and down hills, climb, and exercise small muscles by digging in the sand or playing in water. As they explore the outdoor environment, all children make discoveries about the properties of their world.

Outdoor play and exploration are an essential part of the science curriculum because young children learn through their senses—hearing, smell, taste, touch, and vision. They also learn science concepts through the motoric manipulation of objects. Active experiences outside the school walls provide the opportunity for sensation, observation, and cooperation:

1. ***Sensory experiences.*** Being out-of-doors offers "so many enticing ways to engage the senses! Foods and flowers are great for smells, but so are fresh earth, decaying leaves, and freshly mown grass or hay. Nothing offers as much variety in terms of shapes and colors as the world of nature. The same is true of textures and temperatures" (Wilson, 1995, p. 6).

    Teachers will want to expand water and sand play out-of-doors. As children play with hoses or run through a sprinkler, they explore the properties of water. They can wash doll clothes and hang them in the sun to dry, or hold a car wash and wash all the trikes, wagons, and wheel toys. Adding a trickling water hose and plastic squirt bottles filled with water to the sand area lets children create large structures in the sandbox.

    Digging in the dirt and extracting different sizes of pebbles and rocks is another sensory experience that provides information to the child about the nature of the surfaces of the earth, concepts of heavy and light, rough and smooth, and large and small. Learnings are best reinforced when teachers have questions to focus children on their inquiries. For example, when examining rocks, focusing questions might be "How are they alike/different?" "Which ones are smooth?"

2. ***Observation.*** The natural world is filled with things for children to observe. Clouds, rain, sprouting seeds from a simple class garden, falling leaves, birds, insects, shadows—all are experienced out-of-doors. Teachers will want to encourage children to observe carefully and formulate questions to be answered through active inquiry and discovery. Teachers will record the observations of younger children (who cannot write), while older children can record their observations in a science journal or on chart paper.

3. ***Opportunities to cooperate with others.*** An important part of children's explorations is telling others what they see, what they think, and what further questions

are raised by their experiences. "Children should have lots of time to talk about what they observe and to compare their observations with those of others" (American Association for the Advancement of Science, 1993, p. 6). *Benchmarks for Science Literacy* further suggests that by kindergarten, children should learn to work in small teams (rather than as isolated individuals) to ask and answer questions about their environment. Yet, consistent with the findings of Piaget (1954), it is noted that children learn by reaching different conclusions and working out disagreements about what their findings mean.

Of course, children play cooperatively indoors, but being outside somehow fosters expansive, and often long-term cooperative efforts to construct large buildings and objects, for example. Complex schemes for rearranging equipment, digging gardens, making cities in the sand, and creating areas for the observation of insects and birds develop and bloom out-of-doors. Suggestions for many of these activities are found in the following chapters.

SPACE PLANNING

The out-of-doors is really an extension of the stimulating, well-arranged indoor learning environment. The added richness of natural surroundings and open spaces enhances possibilities for active science learning experiences. Yet, science activities are intimately connected and integrated with all areas of the early childhood curriculum. "This integrated approach to science education weaves physical, sensory, and emotional activities into the total learning process (Harlan & Rivkin, 2000, p. 13)."

Science and Nature Discovery Areas

Spaces should be designated for exploration and discovery. These include the following:

- An area set aside for bird feeders, birdhouses, and birdbaths. Children can observe and record from a distance the comings and goings of a variety of birds, their nests, and the foods that they eat. If they are lucky, it might be possible to observe eggs hatching. The teacher will want to encourage children to listen carefully to the sounds in this area of the play yard. Of course, the type of birds observed will vary with locale and weather conditions.

- An outside sandbox. While an indoor sand table provides children with many active experiences with science, an outside sandbox has many advantages. Children can climb into it, sit in the sand while playing in it, and have the space to create on a large scale. The sand area should be adjacent to a water source. Props for discovering the properties of sand such as colanders, sieves, funnels, small containers, cooking utensils, and sand molds should be added.

- A carefully supervised wading pool or water table. Water play gives children essential skills in pouring, measuring, and comparing. Outside, much more splashing and spilling is acceptable, and water can be carried around the play yard. Many items may be added as required by the type of investigation children are pursuing. For example, water and bubbles illustrate the refraction of light.

- An area where insects and small animals flourish around bushes, plants, and flowers and in the dirt. The life cycle of living things can be directly observed and recorded in photographs, drawings, and graphs. Watching birds, insects, and small animals fosters the concept of the variety of life on earth. "People seem to have a fundamental need to care for things outside themselves. This need can be met—and human life enriched—by caring for the natural world. A genuine concern for wild creatures and their habitats can promote great fulfillment in one's individual life and a sense of caring for other people" (Wilson, 1995, p. 7).

- A garden area for various types of plants, flowers, and vegetables. This space should be carefully placed beyond the limits of children's active play and close to a water source so that very young children can be involved in nurturing the plantings. Some teachers may want to reserve part of the gardening area for impromptu digging where children learn about the composition of soil, the insects and worms that make their homes there, and the organic matter that decomposes to produce soil. The area should be arranged to receive at least six hours of sunlight a day. In locations where this is not possible, teachers should plan gardens that flourish in the shade.

The above are suggestions for a planned approach to using the school yard as a science discovery center. These may be supplemented by carefully chosen field trips. The most effective learning experiences probably occur in the natural environment, which is discussed in a later chapter.

Art Activities

Any art activity can take place outside. From painting with water on school walls or sheds to painting with color on large brown paper strips hanging on a playground fence, children and teachers can enjoy aesthetic experiences with the knowledge that cleanup will be simple. Further, children learn science concepts by experimenting with the properties of water, observing under what conditions water dries, and mixing paints to the desired consistency or colors to the desired hues.

Children can draw on the hard surfaces with large chunk chalk (a form of rock) dipped in water. Their creations will wash away with the next rain. Or they can use crayons or markers on large papers spread on the yard or tables. Modeling with clay and other materials is fun to do outside, as is building with boxes, found objects, and other materials. Through their constructions, children learn about the attributes of things and discover which are effective and ineffective in creating satisfactory structures. Measurement and number are involved in creating structures that work, and when things fall apart, children can make inferences about suitable and unsuitable choices.

Math Activities

Math skills are intimately intertwined with those required for grasping science concepts. Outside, it is possible to use numbers to count things, and place them in order. Children may estimate quantities of rocks or trees by using their observational skills. The smooth stones a child gathers, the acorns another collects, the sticks or plastic cups in the sandbox, the number of children waiting to ride a new trike—all these give children something concrete to count. Children also classify the stones, insects, seeds, and acorns they find, or place them in order from smallest to largest, heaviest to lightest. Shapes such as circles, squares, and triangles can be used to describe many things that can be seen in the play yard, in the natural environment, or in buildings viewed from the outside.

Children learn about math and the physical world through materials, small pieces of equipment, and props that can be moved around and with which they can build and be creative. With movable equipment, children can construct their own play environments using boxes, boards, barrels, tires, and tubes.

Physical Activities

Space and a variety of stationary and movable equipment foster running, jumping and climbing out-of-doors. Experiences with simple machines are also abundant outdoors. Wheeled toys can introduce the principle of the wheel; a seesaw, the lever. Equipment that promotes social interactions, use of language, and cooperative play and is rich with potential for children to form concepts of the physical properties of their world includes the following:

- Large wooden crates and boxes, boards with cleats, and large hollow blocks. The size of these materials demands that two or more children work together to use them for building.

- Climbing equipment that comes in several movable sections, such as a trestle unit, a climbing gate, or an A-frame unit, that can be arranged and rearranged to meet children's changing interest or needs. Playhouses often come designed with storage sheds below.

- Cable tables of assorted sizes, tree trunks with sharp branches removed, and sturdy wooden barrels.

- Balance beams, an old log, several logs placed end to end, a board placed on its side, or stepping stones, patio stones, or old tires placed in a series give children a sense of different ways to handle their bodies in space.

- A wide assortment of balls of all sizes and weights.

- Things to push, pull, and ride. These give children a sense of control over their environment and assist them in learning how things work.

Other Considerations

Ideally, outdoor environments should include sections with different surfaces such as grass, concrete, earth, and sand. Pine bark, cedar chips, or pine needles can be used to create soft areas, while other surfaces can be paved for playing organized games, which give children a sense of using their bodies in space. Play yards should have a balance of sun and shade, active areas for large motor activities, and quiet areas where a child might take a book, listen to music, or play with small manipulatives. Attention should be given to different terrains. A balance of levels can make the play yard visually interesting and provide hills for climbing and rolling down as well as flat surfaces for organized activities. Outdoor pathways wind around the out-of-doors and define various interest areas. They can be created of cedar chips, stones, or cement.

Benchmarks for Science Literacy (American Association for the Advancement of Science, 1993) highlight the importance of tools to scientific inquiry. Teachers will want to add tools such as thermometers, magnifiers, and rulers to aid children in their scientific observations. Simple cameras provide an excellent way for young children to document discoveries in the outdoor environment.

THE TEACHER'S ROLE

Some teachers operate under the mistaken assumption that they are free from any responsibility for children's learning when the class is outside. Yes, there are supervisory and safety considerations, but children are now on their own to let off steam and have a good time. These teachers see outdoor play as a break for them and an opportunity to

> ## GENERAL SAFETY AND HEALTH CONSIDERATIONS FOR ACTIVE OUTDOOR ENVIRONMENTS
>
> - Fencing at least 4 feet high surrounds the play yard.
> - All surfaces are properly maintained and checked for debris such as broken glass and animal waste.
> - All plantings within the fence are nonpoisonous.
> - Play equipment is inspected daily for missing or broken parts, splinters, sharp edges.
> - Sandboxes have a retractable cover.
> - Play area is well drained—water is not allowed to sit.
> - Soil is tested for lead and other toxic substances and fresh soil is brought in for digging and gardens when necessary.
> - Climbing and sliding equipment is anchored firmly in soft ground cover at least 1-foot deep.
> - Equipment is developmentally appropriate (or can be adapted) for the age group/s using it.
> - Railings enclose high equipment to protect from falls.
> - Equipment is spaced for safe movement between pieces.
> - Play yards are accessible to children with disabilities, foster their independence, and enhance skill development.

talk with other adults. "Changing an educational mentality in which children are simply 'let out for recess' and nothing more, thus fostering aggressive unsafe play, is difficult when funds for education are shrinking and other conspicuous needs are emerging. Teachers will make the difference, asserting the essentialness of a safe and challenging outdoors for education and weaving outdoor experiences into their academic curriculum" (Rivkin, 1995, p. 53).

The early childhood science curriculum, perhaps more than other curriculum areas, requires that the teacher take an active role in facilitating children's active "sciencing" through planning and using teaching strategies that "push" children's thinking beyond its current level. Vygotsky's theory suggests that children can be guided by explanation, demonstration, and appropriate questioning to higher conceptual levels through interaction with more capable and competent adults and peers.

Thus, in the outdoor (as well as the indoor) environment, teachers

- engage children actively. They provide many and varied opportunities for observing, communicating, comparing, organizing, and inferring on the basis of active outdoor experiences.

- serve as models displaying the attitudes and skills they want for the children. "Teachers who think that holding worms or mice or observing spiders is distasteful must work to overcome such aversions or to incorporate the content with different examples, such as caterpillars, gerbils, and ants. Teachers are not expected to know all there is to know about sciencing. What is important is that the teacher be open, enthusiastic, and willing to wonder 'What happens if. . .?' " (Kilmer & Hofman, 1995, p. 43).

- enter into joint activities with children, working collaboratively with them on a problem or task, such as building a bird feeder or charting the number and type of birds that are using the feeder.

- assess children's attitudes, skills, and knowledge in the area of science using multiple methods. Through observations of children's work and focused discussions with children, teachers plan for outdoor experiences at the next level of thinking.

- employ appropriate questions and comments to focus children on their scientific inquiries.

SUMMARY

Active outdoor environments for young children enhance the possibilities for learning in all curricular areas; however, natural surroundings and more open spaces are especially important for active "sciencing." Well-planned outdoor environments fulfill important benchmarks for learning by providing young children with sensory experiences, opportunities for observation, and opportunities to cooperate with others and to ask and answer questions about their environment. In science and nature discovery areas, places are planned for observation of birds, insects, and small animals, and exploration of sand and water. Since not everything can be planned outdoors, incidental learnings play a large part, as when a very different type of bird visits the bird feeder in the fall.

A variety of stationary and movable equipment fosters children's physical activity and their understanding of how their bodies move in space. Safety, aesthetics, and balance of environmental factors are taken into consideration when planning for outdoor play and learning. A wide assortment of props and tools aid children in their play and scientific observations. Yet, no outdoor environment is a learning environment without a teacher who is active in planning and encouraging children's concept development.

4

Building Connections to Home and Community Through Active Experiences

Wonderful resources to enhance science education outside the classroom are flourishing in communities throughout the country. Interactive children's science museums, nature centers, zoos, aquariums, and planetariums offer informal science programs for children and families in pleasurable, noncompetitive settings.

Harlan & Rivkin, 2000, p. 26

According to the National Science Education Standards, "The school science program must extend beyond the walls of the school to the resources of the community" (National Research Council, 1996, p. 13). John Dewey believed that schools could not function "when separated from the interest of home and community" (Dewey, 1944, p. 86). He depicted the school at the center with the free interplay of influences, materials, and ideas flowing to both the home and the natural environment around the school building, and back again to life in school. The work of Piaget (Youniss & Damon, 1992) and Vygotsky (Berk & Winsler, 1995) further confirms the importance of building connections to home and community through active experiences.

According to Piaget, "culture acquiring" children construct knowledge about their world by interacting with the environment, peers, and adults in school and beyond the school (Youniss & Damon, 1992). Vygotsky (1978) saw children as learning to think and develop concepts by mastering challenging tasks in collaboration with more knowledgeable members of their society. In addition to teachers, our communities have many specialists that may be available as resources for classes and for individual students. Moreover, many communities have access to science centers, museums, national laboratories, and industry that can contribute greatly to the understanding of science and encourage students to further their interests outside of school. In addition, the physical environment in and around the school can be used as a living laboratory for the study of natural phenomena. "Whether the school is located in a densely populated urban area, a sprawling suburb, a small town, or a rural area, the environment can and should be used as a resource for science study" (National Research Council, 1996, p. 13).

Working with others in their school and with the community, teachers will want to build these resources into their interactions with children. Thus, the immediate environment of the school and community serves as a laboratory or workshop for children to discover the world around them and the people and things that populate that world. Without these active experiences, children lack the raw materials to construct learnings in the classroom that have meaning and integrity. Children are cheated when teachers provide pictures of birds, insects, and trees and expect children to form concepts from these instead of observing them in the world outside the school. In addition to observation, in the natural environment children may engage in the science process skills of comparing, counting, classifying, defining, communicating, hypothesizing, predicting, testing, and experimenting.

In his ecological approach, Bronfenbrenner (1979) placed the developing child in the center of a series of interlocking settings. Home, school, and the neighborhood serve as the immediate basis for child development and learning. Just as active children derive meaning from their experiences in the classroom, that meaning is extended and broadened when teachers recognize the family as a resource for deep and personally meaningful learning experiences.

Mr. Porter, a teacher of 4-year-olds, had attended some summer workshops on the teaching of science and became convinced that it was necessary for him to build connections with the home and wider community through well-planned excursions. Using his experience from the workshops, and the help of his colleagues, he formulated the following criteria for experiences with integrity and meaning:

•   There is a continuity of experience as one builds upon another. Mr. Porter had some difficulty with the policy of his school to take a field trip each week to a different place, and realized that the children were having a series of isolated experiences that were soon forgotten. Instead, to build experiences around one theme or concept area would help children construct knowledge in depth and to generalize it to other areas.

•   Each experience is worth the child's and teacher's time and effort. A trip to the university laboratory had been long and exhausting. The exhibits had been placed too high for most children to see or touch. Worse, the student in charge was not used to young children and lectured them as she did secondary students. The children whined, fidgeted, and started poking and fighting with one another. Later, when asked what they remembered about the trip, the children talked only about the drinking fountains.

•   Advanced organizers should be provided for the children. Children need opportunities to discuss, read about, and role-play the excursion in advance. Some teachers find that asking children to make a list of what they already know, what they want to see, and what they think they will see on the trip is helpful. After a walk in the park, for example, children could compare their list with the actual experience.

•   Children should have time to reflect upon and follow up on experiences with plans and projects that enhance and expand their learning.

•   A planned experience should either be an outgrowth of children's deep interests or meet a specific need for the children in learning subject matter content. One of Mr. Porter's colleagues was teaching her class of 3-year-olds about electricity. They seemed to be having a good time playing with small bulbs, batteries, and wires. Yet, when asked what they were learning, they told him, "Magic." At first confused, Mr. Porter soon understood that this abstract concept (electricity) had not been made concrete for the children, nor did the activities have personal meaning for them.

•   Flexibility is essential. While most outside experiences are well planned in advance, teachers can capitalize on incidental learnings, such as when children spot a nest of baby birds, find a spiderweb in the outside playhouse, or find interesting and colorful rocks.

OUT INTO THE SCHOOL

Now, where can the teacher and children find the active experiences that build connections to home and community and take them outside the classroom walls?

Whether a kindergarten or a Head Start program in a large elementary school, a child-care center or a small cooperative nursery school, there are many meaningful ways to utilize the immediate environment of the building itself and the grounds that surround it.

Inside the School Building

There are many active experiences for children when they take a walk around the school building. Children are intensely interested in machines and tools that help us do work. Children who are in an elementary school setting can meet with the secretary, the nurse, a custodian, an office worker, the persons who pick up the garbage, and the cook. The teacher might assist the children in preparing a list of questions to ask by getting them to think about the jobs that people do and what tools they need to perform their tasks. Large and small machinery may be observed and described. Children may be asked to speculate what different kinds of tools are used by persons who work in the school such as hammers, saws, pliers, screwdrivers, nails, scissors, staplers, eggbeaters, thermometers, scales, flashlights, and word processors. These learnings can be expanded in the classroom as tools are provided for children in various centers of interest.

Outside in the Natural Environment

Studies of children's knowledge of the plants and animals in their environment reveals that they know much less than older people in their culture group, although Native American children were more knowledgeable than Anglo children (Rivkin, 1995). The immediate outdoor environment of the school provides children with a rich laboratory for studying nature and their physical world. They should be encouraged to think of all the things they can observe and be prepared by the teacher to observe closely and to gather and record data on flowers, trees, small animals, weather, sounds, and seasons. "By exploring in the out-of-doors, children learn about the physical characteristics of the natural world—e.g., the hardness of a rock, the stability of a tree, the fragility of an eggshell or spiderweb, and the smoothness of an apple. Through hands-on manipulations, children discover that some things are heavy and others are light; water can spread out over the sidewalk or soak down into the ground" (Wilson, p. 5).

OUT INTO THE NEIGHBORHOOD AND COMMUNITY

Ms. Smith, a teacher of 3-year-olds in a childcare center, had heard how wonderful the regional park was. Yes, it was a 45-minute trip, but it would be worth it for the children to experience the small farm and petting zoo and to talk to the rangers.

She planned to entertain them on the bus with finger plays and songs, and the assisting parents would enjoy it too. It started well. Everyone was enjoying the ride and began singing "The Wheels on the Bus." That is, until several children became ill. Things went downhill from there. Children cried. The adults, exhausted from trying to comfort the children, became cross. On the return trip, everyone was anxious to see the familiar grounds of the center.

What went wrong here? First, was the trip meaningful, or was it a waste of valuable time and resources? Ms. Smith thought hard about these questions. She soon understood that the trip was not appropriate for the developmental level of the children in her classroom, although it could have been an excellent experience for older children. Her 3-year-olds could find many experiences with life sciences right in their own play yard.

In planning for meaningful experiences for children, teachers prepare the children, but they also prepare themselves. The purpose of a trip is to provide children with firsthand experiences based on their interests that they would be unable to have in the classroom, in school, or on the immediate grounds. In fact, the first step for the teacher might be to decide if the purpose could be accomplished another way. Do the children need to go to the science museum, or would it be possible to bring science resource persons into the school to plan experiments and pose problems? If school visits are not possible, the teacher decides on the goals and then plans for experiences prior to, during, and after the trip.

Teachers will want to become familiar with the community and its resources prior to planning any trip. Unforeseen difficulties can be avoided if teachers preview the site and talk with the people at the places they wish to visit such as the nature center or the children's museum. Some sites such as museums and libraries have prepared tours and materials for children; however, these may be too long or complex for very young children. Teachers should shorten and modify an experience when necessary and create their own materials that will be age appropriate.

Teachers will also want to consider the integrative power of a field trip (Seefeldt, 1997). How will the science trip facilitate growth in the language arts, mathematics, and the use of books, writing, the arts, and social skills? As teachers prepare the children, they will emphasize active experiences in all of these areas. In addition, they will choose children's literature that integrates science throughout the early childhood curriculum. Each active experience will involve learning new vocabulary words and investigating the site through informational books and fiction. Children will want to draw pictures, dictate stories, and sing songs about what they have done. They will re-create and reinvent their learnings through dramatic play inside and outside the classroom. Social skills develop as children experience new people and places and acquire behaviors to fit the situation.

BASIC GUIDELINES FOR MEANINGFUL FIELD EXPERIENCES

1. Keep the experience simple for very young children, and increase the complexity as it is developmentally appropriate. For example, very young children will profit from a short walk to collect leaves in the fall. With the teacher's help, they may classify the leaves first by color and then by shape. Older children will advance their concept of the relationship between food and health by visiting the food store to select items that correspond to the sections of the food pyramid.

2. Consider the mode of transportation. Walking is best for most children, yet some field trips necessitate bus or public transportation. In fact, when learning about gears and wheels, a trip on the bus is an authentic and active experience.

3. If the classroom is inclusive, consider all aspects of the field experience. Pathways and sites must be barrier free and experiences must be open-ended so that all children profit from the trip. Small group excursions may provide a better opportunity for all learners to profit.

4. Introduce the field experience through discussions, pictures, reading about the things to be viewed, and art experiences. For example, if children are to visit botanical gardens, they may observe, compare, and describe the many plants they find in the play yard; plant a seed and observe the effects of water and light on its growth; cut pictures from magazines of beautiful or exotic plants and make a collage; read about plants that grow in different types of soil, and even vote on their favorite plant. Small group work in areas of particular interest should be encouraged.

SOME SAFETY TIPS FOR FIELD EXPERIENCES

- Obtain parental permission for children to participate in the excursion.
- Check the environment ahead, both inside and out, for any hazards.
- Be sure all teachers and staff members are trained in first aid and CPR.
- Include at least one person with such training on the trip.
- Take a first-aid kit on the excursion.
- Take an up-to-date list of emergency phone numbers for each child.
- Check medical forms for children's allergies (including reactions to wasp and bee stings and foods).
- Always walk on the left, facing traffic.
- Be sure that children understand that small wild animals are for observation and not handling.
- Educate children about poisonous plants and drinking water from streams in the outdoor environment.
- When utilizing transportation, make sure the children know, have practiced, and will follow the rules.
- Consider adult/child ratios. Include no more than three or four children on a field trip for each adult present and fewer if the trip requires complex arrangements for transportation.
- Remember that small group excursions may be best for all learners.
- Be sure the field trip site meets guidelines for children who are developmentally different.

---

5. Organize play around the places to be visited. The creative dramatic center and the outside environment can be adapted to fit science field experiences. Often additional clothes or props will be needed. Young children wear lab coats and carry simple equipment for collecting specimens for science classes at the Lawrence Hall of Sciences in Berkeley, California.

6. Prepare the children to observe closely and gather data during the field trip. Their observations will be used as the basis for many activities in the days and weeks to follow. For example, children have probably been on walks many times with their parents. Yet, they have not paid close attention to the smells, shapes, variety, and colors of the trees and others plants that line their way. Questions originating from older children may be compiled on sheets to remind them of the experiences they wish to have.

7. Give children plenty of opportunities to reflect on their experiences. Allot time and materials for follow-up plans and projects. Isolated experiences are easily forgotten. Learnings from field trips are part of an integrated curriculum.

8. Welcome parents during any phase of the planning, implementation, or follow-up. Opportunities for parent participation should accommodate parents' schedules. Parents need not come to the school or field experience. There are many ways they can enhance their children's experiences in the home if they are informed of the teachers' plans and activities.

BUILDING CONNECTIONS WITH THE NEIGHBORHOOD AND COMMUNITY

According to Swick (1997), "Communities offer multiple opportunities to extend and enrich children's conceptions of work. Learning to take care of the environment is a priority for today's children and an inviting place to connect work and human functioning" (p. 39). Adopting a stream or a playground gives children a sense of responsibility and participation in society through real-life experiences. In our throwaway culture, young children can learn environmental values. Additional ways to introduce children to science through community responsibility and caring include visits to a veterinary clinic and carefully facilitated intergenerational contacts.

Mr. Vasquez noticed that the 5-year-olds he taught were treating classroom animals carelessly. He decided to plan several trips to the local veterinarian to foster empathy and understanding in children. He believed that in the process of learning how to care properly for a small animal, they would expand their knowledge and develop respect and appreciation for all living things. He noticed improvement at the outset, and by the end of the visits, children were volunteering to care for the classroom animals and setting careful rules.

Through carefully planned intergenerational programs, children and elders interact with one another, reestablishing the relationships of caring and continuity of life that have been broken by physical and social distance. The teacher will want to plan programs and contacts carefully since children tend to hold negative stereotypes about the elderly and in some instances fear contacts. With this is mind, it would be unwise to take children to nursing homes where elders have symptoms of senility and infirmity.

Seefeldt (1997) suggests that when children are exposed to elders who are healthy, happy, active, and fulfilled, they can share the love of an older person: "Intergenerational programs in the school can provide a way for children and elders to enjoy one another's company, to learn from one another, to share feelings of affection, and to provide children with a concrete example of life's continuity" (p. 195).

Every community has natural resources, people resources, and material resources. The teachers will want to make an effort to become acquainted with these resources to extend and expand the science offerings possible in the classroom.

Natural Resources

Parks and nature centers offer extra glimpses into the world of woods, trees, plants, ponds, lakes, beaches, animals, birds, and the like. The National Park Service runs a number of centers that have "hands-on" science activities for children, trails to follow with guides written for children, and knowledgeable rangers to pose and answer children's questions. The ranger or guide may have a snake on hand or an active animal shelter to show. Local communities also sponsor park and recreational services for children.

Visitors

Visitors who enhance the science curriculum include parents and other specialists in transportation, health-care delivery, computer technologies, music, art, cooking, mechanics, and many other fields that have scientific aspects. They can be effective resource people if the teacher prepares the children carefully for their visits, and encourages them to provide active demonstrations or "hands-on" opportunities.

Zoos

Zoos are controversial in the science and environmental community because they remove animals from their natural surroundings and, until recently in this country, relied on fences and other restraints to separate the animals from their visitors. More recently, zoos have become more aware of concerns for animals and employ more natural barriers, fewer cages, and appropriate habitats for the animals. There are many good zoos with highly trained docents and guides to work with children. At the National Zoo in Washington, DC, the volunteers who work with children must take a rigorous course of study in both animal life and how to teach life science effectively to children. Excellent written materials enhance the child's visit with questions and comments to promote scientific thinking and invitations to make drawings and write stories about the animals. The zoo staff will hang the children's pictures and stories where they can be viewed by other young visitors.

Science Centers and Museums

Most science centers and museums have planned activities for children including experiments and opportunities to handle small creatures. At the Lawrence Hall of Science, young children are invited to don a lab coat and go down to the pond to collect tadpoles. The specimens are arranged with the children's names and are observed over time. At the Smithsonian Institution in Washington, DC, "Don't Touch" has been replaced by "Please Handle with Care" in the discovery areas of the museum. Trained persons supervise the handling of fragile shells and nonpoisonous insects.

Other community resources that teachers may want to consider are

- colleges and universities

- radio or television stations

- transportation services such as airports and train stations

- professional services such as doctors' offices and hospitals

- commercial services such as bakeries, pharmacies, factories, and farms

- observatories

- aquariums

THE HOME-SCHOOL CONNECTION

The family has long been considered the child's first and foremost teacher and possibly the child's primary community for learning (Bredekamp & Copple, 1997; Powell, 1989). Teachers can utilize the family as a resource for children's learning both in the school and in the home. There is an increased research base on the benefits to the child of family involvement even if the extent of that involvement is small (Grolnick & Slowiaczek, 1994; Marcon, 1992; Stevenson & Baker, 1987).

Teachers and parents may face some challenges in working together. According to Powell (1989), early childhood educators increasingly service families characterized by single-parents households, cultural diversity and ethnic minority status, dual-worker or dual-career lifestyles, economic pressures, and geographic mobility. The new demographics of family structure call into question the viability of existing approaches to relations between families and early childhood programs. Yet, frequent contacts cement a genuine respect and tolerance for different family types. Involving parents as active partners in the classroom provides both parent and teacher with firsthand information about the expectations of the home and the school.

Classrooms work best and children learn more when parents are involved. Teachers may employ the following multiple approaches:

- Conferences in which teachers provide parents with samples of children's work and invite parents to share their observations about their children's learning and their suggestions for classroom and community experience based on their children's interests.

- Use of informal contacts. Busy parents enjoy a brief chat before school, telephone calls, informal notes, and bulletin boards that inform them of plans and programs and invite them to participate in a variety of ways.

- Somewhat more formal contacts through the provision of a Parents' Corner or Family Room where parents may interact around learning materials and other activities of interest to the family. Often these include a lending library with toys and picture and reference books.

- Regular newsletters explaining the goals for the week, why certain activities were planned, and how parents can support the lessons at home. Other items to include in newsletters are special events at school, science activities that children have enjoyed, special television programs on scientific topics that parents and children might watch together, and special events for children and families occurring in the community.

- An open-door policy for parent observation and participation. If parents are unable to work regularly as paid or unpaid volunteers, they may make or send materials for special projects in the classroom, help on field trips, or come to school when their schedules permit.

- Selection of active science experiences for children that can be documented. Children will have products such as drawings, charts, or stories to communicate to busy parents what they are doing in school.

Parents support the teaching of science by the interactions they have with their children at home. Brewer (1998) suggests that teachers "help parents understand that children learn science when they wash a greasy dish, water a garden plot, ride their trike down a sloped surface, and so on. Some parents think science experiences have to be formal and difficult for learning to occur" (p. 344). Additionally, by learning about the diverse cultures of their students' families, teachers can avoid science activities that will be offensive such as experimenting with food or studying animals that have symbolic meaning in a culture.

Parents can encourage scientific thinking in their children by asking open-ended questions and taking time to encourage the answers. They can help their children to observe ("What shapes do you see on that tree?"), classify ("Let's put away your toys by color"), predict ("How long will it take that squirrel to get up the tree?"), and quantify ("How tall is that building?"). It is possible to practice the skills of science everywhere (National Science Teacher's Association, 1999.) In addition, it is never too early for parents to encourage children to care for the environment.

Teachers will want to plan family science events at school and send suggestions home in the class newsletter for supporting science learnings in the home. Successful school science events will involve the whole family in collecting data, undertaking investigations, and solving puzzles and problems. These are active experiences for the whole family. The standard school science fair usually involves complex materials and equipment and seems more like a competition than a joint exploration that is both fun and intellectually stimulating. The following interactions with parents should introduce them to, and involve them in, children's science experiences:

1. In the class newsletter, have a weekly suggestion box designed for supplementing the science curriculum at home. For example, highlight free activities occurring in the community, exhibits to be visited, activities based on kitchen science, and backyard activities.

2. Have parents and children work together to create minimuseums at home that can be shared with the class when completed. Send parents a note explaining the goal of the activity, how it is related to work at school, and simple directions for making the minimuseum. An example might be a collection of shells from a visit to the beach.

3. Teachers may want to put together a "science backpack" that children take home on a rotating basis (Brewer, 1998). The backpack contains a note explaining the purpose of the activity, an information book related to the activity, and all the materials necessary for completing the activity. The teacher will want to make sure that all of the materials contained in the backpack are easy and fun for parents to use and are translated into their native language.

Additionally, even if family members cannot volunteer in the classroom on a regular basis, they can share their talents, occupations, hobbies, customs, and traditions with the class and school community as they are able.

SUMMARY

Building and maintaining connections with home and community provide benefits to all. Young children need active experiences consistent with their participation in science education. These experiences require careful planning by teachers, who are rewarded by observing children's authentic learning, as one experience builds upon another into an integrated whole. As the family is recognized as a valuable resource for learning, parents and teachers feel mutually supported and learn to understand and value each other as contributors to the child's understanding of science. All of this is consistent with a strong emphasis on "sciencing" in the curriculum for young children.

5

Experiences and Science Content

From the earliest grades, students should experience science in a form that engages them in the active construction of ideas and explanations that enhance their opportunities to develop the abilities of doing science as inquiry, provides teachers with the opportunity to develop students' abilities and to enrich student understanding of science. Students should do science in ways that are within their developmental capabilities.

National Research Council, 1996, p. 121

Firsthand experiences in their classrooms, homes, and communities form the foundation for children's learning. These are like the first rungs on the learning ladder. But unless a firsthand experience leads children to an ever-expanding world of new facts, information, and knowledge previously unfamiliar, children's learning will be limited. Thus, the next step on the learning ladder is the expansion and extension of the knowledge children have gained through their firsthand experiences into a fuller, richer, thicker, and more organized form (Dewey, 1938). This form will gradually approximate the experts' understanding of a given subject matter or content area.

KNOWLEDGE OF CHILDREN

Knowledge of some of the universals of children's growth, development, and learning is necessary for the teacher to capitalize on and plan experiences that are both developmentally appropriate and challenge the limits of children's understanding. There is a wide variation, however, in children's growth, development, and learning. Some is due to the variation in the sociocultural context of children's lives; some to the variation in patterns of normal growth and development.

Even though each preschool child is unique, we know from research and theory that children around the same age view the world around them from similar perspectives and can profit from science content that is geared to their general level of development. This is why the National Science Education Standards (National Research Council, 1996) and the Benchmarks for Science Literacy (American Association for the Advancement of Science, 1993) suggest that progress toward their standards or goals is developmental. Most of the basic skills and concepts can be introduced to preschoolers and expanded upon through kindergarten and the early primary grades. "Children who have many interesting, direct experiences over time with science concepts will gradually understand the broader principles as they develop the cognitive skills to make more abstract generalizations" (Kilmer & Hofman, 1995, p. 47).

There are many resources teachers can use to gain a better understanding of children's general growth and development. Authorities in the field of early childhood education such as Bredekamp and Copple, who edited *Developmentally Appropriate Practice in Early Childhood Programs* (1997), have identified universal patterns of children's growth, development, and learning.

This universal information about children's growth and development informs teachers about the potentials and vulnerabilities of young children. This knowledge tells us that in general, the younger the child, the more wedded the child is to learning through firsthand interactions with the environment and others. Three-, four-, and five-year-olds, still in Piaget's preoperational period of cognitive development and busy actively constructing their own knowledge, must rely on firsthand experiences in order to learn. As they grow and mature, however, they become increasingly more reliant on interpreting and extending their experiential learning through symbols, through pictures, and through spoken and written language.

KNOWLEDGE OF THE SUBJECT MATTER—SCIENCE

Knowledge of children alone is not enough if teachers are to expand and extend children's learning. If teachers are to take children further up the learning ladder, then they must also have a solid understanding of the subject matter they want children to learn.

Just as authorities in the field of early childhood have identified universals of children's growth, development, and learning, so authorities in the field of science have identified general facts, information, and knowledge key to science for young children (American Association for the Advancement of Science, 1993; National Research Council, 1996). Knowledge of these key concepts, themes, and standards that serve to organize science education guides teachers in the selection of firsthand experiences that will serve as a base for children's learning, as well as lead them in expanding and extending these firsthand experiences into more formal, conventional knowledge.

Many teachers report that they feel less prepared to teach science than any other subject matter area (Wenner, 1993). It appears that such feelings result from teachers' misconceptions that science for children requires a command of difficult concepts and facts, expensive and complicated materials, and an emphasis on student memorization and acquisition of facts. This view of science has changed. During the last two decades, a number of researchers have focused on how children learn. Early childhood educators now believe that children are constructive learners, constantly creating and constructing their knowledge about the world based on their own questions (Barclay & Traser, 1999). From this perspective, children are natural scientists.

Kilmer and Hofman (1995) believe that "the contribution of early childhood education toward scientific literacy is to lay a solid foundation for the continuing development of an interest in and understanding of science and technology by ensuring that every child—regardless of gender, racial or cultural background or disabilities—actively participates in science experiences and views himself as successful in this endeavor" (p. 44). They use the term "sciencing," which refers to the child's active participation in learning about science and points out the emphasis on process. "Sciencing" is a "hands-on, brains-on" endeavor. They identify the following three goals for "sciencing" with young children:

- To develop each child's innate curiosity about the world.

- To broaden each child's procedural and thinking skills for investigating the world, solving problems, and making decisions.

- To increase each child's knowledge of the natural world.

In general terms, science is now defined as the process of manipulating, observing, thinking, and reflecting on actions and events. The role of experience is primary. The National Science Education Standards view science as inquiry and state that "as students focus on the processes of doing investigations, they develop the ability to ask scientific questions, investigate aspects of the world around them, and use their observations to construct reasonable explanations for the questions posed" (National Research Council, 1996, p. 121).

The Standards emphasize that the teaching of science as inquiry provides teachers with the opportunity to develop student abilities and enrich students' understanding of science, while at the same time adhering to developmental appropriateness. Young children are able to begin the process of full inquiry, which involves asking a question, completing an investigation, answering the question, forming generalizations, and presenting the results to others. Documentation and reflection complete the process.

ORGANIZING CHILDREN'S EXPERIENCES

Organizing children's experiences around some general themes identified by the Benchmarks for Science Literacy and the National Science Education Standards makes the task of the teacher seem less overwhelming. The following themes expressed by both documents serve to organize this book as follows:

1. *Life Science and the Living Environment:* Science programs for young children should provide for direct experience with living things, their life cycles, and their habitats. Although confused at first, young children develop concepts of living and nonliving things, the variety of living things on earth, the process of categorizing living things, the behavior and needs of living things (including their environments), and respect for living things.

    The emergent themes of the life sciences are reflected in experience 1, "Living Things Grow and Change: Seeds and Plants," and experience 2, "Living Things: Insects and Small Animals," of this book. Concepts involved in exploring the natural world are embedded in these experiences.

2. *Earth Science and the Physical Setting:* Young children are naturally interested in everything they see around them—soil, rocks, streams, rain, sand, and shells. Science should include experiences that provide for the study of the properties of earth materials, and the discovery of patterns and changes in water, rocks, and minerals. They are intensely interested in the outdoor environment, naturally use it as a laboratory for learning, and enjoy drawing or recording/charting what they see and think both individually and in small groups.

    The themes that emerge from the study of earth science are reflected in experience 5, "The Earth: Water," and experience 6, "The Earth: Rocks and Minerals," in this book.

3. *Science in Personal and Social Perspectives and the Human Organism:* While young children can't grasp many of the abstractions inherent in this category, central ideas related to learning through the senses and mental and physical health provide the foundations for students' eventual understandings and individual and collective actions as citizens. Concepts and attitudes about personal and collective health and nutrition are essential for well-being. An understanding of how one brings in information through the senses expands children's observational skills and permits the processes of investigating the world, solving problems, and reaching conclusions to occur.

    Health, nutrition, and learning through sensory experiences are reflected in experience 7, "The Human Body: The Senses," and experience 8, "Healthy Bodies," in this book.

4. *Physical Science, the Physical Setting and the Designed World:* A science program for young children should include many opportunities for children to exercise their natural curiosity in observing and manipulating common objects and materials in their environment. As children explore the properties of objects and materials (size, weight, shape, and color), they can measure these properties using first simple and then more conventional tools. Beginning concepts develop as young children act on objects to produce a desired effect by putting objects together to form constructions of various kinds and draw conclusions about how the desired effect was produced.

    Themes that emerge from the physical sciences are reflected in experience 3, "I Am a Scientist," and experience 4, "How Toys Work," in this book.

BRINGING KNOWLEDGE OF CHILDREN AND CONTENT TOGETHER

To bring children and science concepts together, teachers first need to find out all they can about the science content they are planning to teach young children. To do so they might do the following:

- Read informational books for adults and children on the subject they want to teach young children. (See experiences 1–8 for references.)

- Determine the underlying concepts that children can learn. Key concepts can be identified through inquiry into authentic questions generated from student experiences and use of major themes generated by the Science Teaching Standards, the Benchmarks for Science Literacy, and knowledge of child growth and development. When a teacher is unsure of a concept and how to make it accessible to young children, she might read books on the topic written for students in the primary grades and adapt key concepts for younger children.

- Ask authorities in the field to share their information and expertise. Professors at nearby colleges and universities are anxious to share their resources with classroom teachers.

- Work collaboratively with other teachers through associations and workshops. Associations such as the National Association for the Education of Young Children, the Association for Childhood Education International, and the National Science Teachers Association hold national and local meetings, publish journals and resource catalogues, and have local chapters.

- Visit museums, watch videos or television, and search the Web.

- Develop a repertoire of questions and comments to promote scientific thinking in children such as "Does _____ look the same today as it did last week?"

Then teachers need to find out what children already know and understand of the concepts key to science themes. To do so, teachers can do the following:

- Interview children. For example, to find out what they know about water, ask them to

  - tell everything they know about water

  - draw a picture about water

  - construct a web with "water words"

  - explain some of the reasons why water is important to life on earth

- Take a walk around a child's neighborhood to understand what the child has already experienced and how these experiences can be expanded into conventional knowledge.

- Talk to a child's family, asking about family experiences, what the child is interested in and likes doing, and what the child is not familiar with or needs to become familiar with.

- Observe children as they work and play, noting what themes are involved in their play and how they solve problems, use language, and interact with others and their world.

EXPANDING AND EXTENDING FIRSTHAND EXPERIENCES

Children's experiences with their world enable them to develop spontaneous, everyday concepts. This everyday, personal knowledge, however, does not automatically lead to a deeper understanding or more conventional ways of knowing. Rather these concepts act like Velcro, hooking onto whatever new information, facts, and experiences children are given. The richer the new information, the greater the possibility for children to see the relationship of one fact to others and to form generalizations.

Vygotsky (1986) pointed out that at different developmental stages, children learn different things as they independently act on and interpret their environment, but also other people interact with children, affecting the course of their development and learning. He thought children operated at two levels of thought. One was the stage at which they could solve problems and think without the guidance of an adult or a more skilled peer. The second level was the stage at which the child could perform a task with adult help or guidance. He called this the potential developmental level. The distance between the two levels was termed the "zone of proximal development" (Vygotsky, 1986).

This means that by understanding children's existing ideas and science content, teachers can extend and expand children's knowledge by doing the following:

- Providing children with all kinds of books—poetry, literature, single-concept picture, and reference books—that pertain to concepts children are studying. Books displaying beautiful photographs of insects and small animals come close to providing a child with the real experience. Children's literature is a valuable science tool. It generates interest and motivation, provides context, invites communication, and connects science with the rest of the child's world (Barclay, Benelli, & Schoon, 1999). Books may be openly displayed on a shelf or table, inviting children to extend and expand their ideas. Some of the books children can use independently; others can be read to the entire group or to an individual child or two.

- Looking at pictures and other print media with children. Videos, photographs, movies, slides, and computer simulations of things in, or not in, their environment, can be examined and discussed to extend and expand children's knowledge.

- Showing children how they can do something. Teachers, working collaboratively with children, can demonstrate how to plant a seed for optimal growth, observe a rock with a magnifier, or record the progress of a bird's nest.

- Telling children a fact or piece of information that will enable them to make sense of their world. Giving children the proper words for scientific phenomena is something that teachers do to enhance learning. There is no way for children to construct these for themselves.

- Questioning children. Ask children what a thing is, why it is this way, and how it got this way to spur their thinking in a new or different way. Questions and comments are key to promoting scientific thinking. When children encounter new materials and phenomena, teachers may need to intervene to focus and challenge students or the exploration might not lead to learning. Premature intervention, however, may deprive students of the opportunity to confront problems and find solutions (National Research Council, 1996).

- Asking children to observe and listen to authorities show or tell about their field: A docent at the Smithsonian Institution can explain the features of rocks and minerals; a park ranger can reveal some of the mysteries of nature during a walk on the nature trail.

- Having children use the computer to learn a new skill or fact, find information, or communicate with others. When utilizing computer software, teachers will want to apply the criteria of age appropriateness, child control, clear instructions, and expanding complexity.

- Adding another experience. Based on an understanding of children's ideas and concepts in the area of science, add another real-life experience that will expand and extend these.

- Providing multiple opportunities for children to learn from one another. Children should be able to revisit their existing ideas of the subject matter by freely sharing their view of the world with others and arguing their point of view. Only through interactions with others can children critically consider their existing ideas, and revise these to form more complex and conventional concepts of their world.

- Modeling the skills of scientific inquiry. "Teachers who exhibit enthusiasm and interest and who speak to the power and beauty of scientific understanding instill in their students some of those same attitudes toward science. Teachers whose actions demonstrate respect for differing ideas, attitudes, and values support a disposition fundamental to science and to science classrooms that also is important in many everyday situations" (National Research Council, 1996).

By respecting the children, how they learn, and the subject matter of the sciences, teachers extend and expand children's existing knowledge. Teachers teach. They also provide time, space, and materials to promote inquiry. Bredekamp and Rosegrant (1995) ask teachers "not to water down the learning experience even for the youngest child" (p. 22), but rather to build on children's existing knowledge and experience, continuously assessing and supporting learning.

SUMMARY

Firsthand experiences enable children to construct everyday, spontaneous concepts. These concepts are like the first rung on a ladder of learning. The role of the teacher is to extend and expand these concepts into fuller, richer, more conventional knowledge. Teachers do this by developing an understanding of children and how they learn and a knowledge of science content, and then bringing the two together.

Authorities in the field of science education have identified themes or concepts key to the field. These are used by teachers to guide them as they extend and expand children's everyday concepts.

Concepts can be expanded and extended in a number of ways. Books, print media, field experiences, the computer, and other technologies can be made available. Teachers can demonstrate skills or apply concepts and provide children with the information that will enable them to reach a fuller understanding of the natural world and the scientific principles needed to understand it.

PART TWO

Guides to Active Experiences

EXPERIENCE

1

Living Things Grow and Change: Seeds and Plants

FOR THE TEACHER

◇ What You'll Need to Know

Since young children are natural investigators, they are anxious to learn about the living things around them. Investigations into seeds and plants provide children with the foundation necessary to study the life cycle in animals and human beings. Developmental psychologists have found that children's understanding of the biological sciences develops gradually. The National Science Education Standards (National Academy of Sciences, 1995) note that young children have basic confusions about living and nonliving and tend to equate life with movement. Further, young children believe that all objects are "made for" a purpose.

Attempting to change children's understanding of the world through direct instruction does not seem to work (Seefeldt, 1998). From a constructivist perspective, children are actively engaged in building theories about the world and the way it works. If teachers believe that children must actively construct their own knowledge, they will not *tell* them about science concepts. The teacher's role is to help children learn science through appropriate planning and through questions and comments that promote scientific thinking. "Inquiry into authentic questions generated from student experiences is the central strategy for teaching science" (National Academy of Sciences, 1995, p. 5). The key to effective science teaching is an emphasis on the process skills of observing, classifying, comparing, predicting, and communicating. Gradually, through active experiences with plant life, children will form the foundation on which later abstract learning can be built.

◇ Key Concepts

- Plants require air, water, food, and light to live.
- There are many kinds of plants, and each has its own form or structure.
- Plants make seeds.
- Seeds grow into plants with roots, stems, leaves, and flowers.
- Plants grow and change.

◇ Goals and Objectives

Children will explore seeds and plants both outside and in the classroom.

Children will identify the processes that permit plants to live.

Children will observe, compare, and classify/measure a variety of seeds.

Children will observe, compare, and classify/measure a variety of plants.

Children will match plants with the seeds that they make.

Children will begin to observe the growth of seeds into plants.

Children will observe how plants change as they grow.

Children will learn scientific terminology for their observations as appropriate.

◇ What You'll Need

You may want to refresh your memory about seeds and plants by consulting "The Outstanding Science Trade Books for Children—1999" (books published in 1998). This list is a cooperative project between the National Science Teachers Association and the

Children's Book Council (see information on access in the Resources section). The following have resources on plants and seeds:

1. *Autumn Leaves* written and illustrated with photographs by Ken Robbins (Scholastic). Takes the reader on a walking tour of some of the most well known autumn leaves and the trees from which they fall. The book features striking color photographs.

2. *Garden* written and illustrated with photographs by Robert Maass (Henry Holt). Depicts the beauty and diversity of gardens. Includes information on the basic care of a garden through the seasons.

3. *National Audubon Society First Field Guide: Wild Flowers* by Anne Rockwell (Walker). Includes a story of what happens to one small bean when it interacts with some soil, just a little water, sunlight, and a child's tender care.

4. *Our Wet World* by Sneed B. Collard (Charlesbridge). Depicts the flora and fauna that inhabit the waterways of our planet.

5. *Buried Treasure: Roots and Tubers* by Meredith Sayles Hughes and Tom Hughes (Lerner). Emphasizes food, observations, and simple experiments, which can be adapted for younger children.

Another good reference book for teachers is *Fostering a Sense of Wonder During the Early Childhood Years* by Ruth Wilson (Greyden).

Children's Books

Baldwin, A. N. (1970). *Sunflowers for Tina.* New York: Scholastic.

Berenstain, S. (1996). *The Berenstain bears grow it: Mother Nature has such a green thumb.* New York: Random House.

Carle, E. (1990). *The tiny seed.* New York: Simon and Shuster.

Carlstrom, N. (1989). *Wild, wild sunflower child Anna.* New York: Macmillan.

Florian, D. (1991). *Vegetable garden.* San Diego, CA: Harcourt Brace Jovanovich.

Gibbons, G. (1993). *From seed to plant.* New York: Holiday House.

Graves, K. (1994). *Is it alive?* Cypress, CA: Creative Teaching Press.

Raffi. (1997). *Everything grows.* New York: Macmillan.

Other Things You'll Need

- A variety of seeds (flower, fruit, and vegetable seeds; birdseed; seeds from trees such as fir cones, acorns, and chestnuts)

- Easily sprouting seeds such as black-eyed pea, lentil, lima bean, corn, pea, pumpkin, marigold, sunflower, and grass

- An assortment of fresh flowers and leaves; and an assortment of dried flowers and leaves

- Nonliving things such as marbles, rocks, and stones

- Photographs and posters of flowers, plants, and trees at different periods of their seasonal cycle

- Large containers for planting and exhibitions
- Plastic or paper plates
- Magnifying glasses
- Soil or sand (indoors or out-of-doors)
- Watering cans
- Measuring tools
- Paper, glue, drawing tools, and other art supplies
- Access to the out-of-doors as a laboratory

◇ The Home-School Connection

There are many ways that parents can assist children with science experiences with seeds and plants. First, they can encourage scientific thinking by asking open-ended questions and taking time for children to formulate the answers. They can also foster the skills of science by inviting young eyes and fingers to notice small details as they take a walk through the park, helping children to put things in groups based on their characteristics, testing children's ideas about how the world works, and encouraging children to quantify the world around them (National Science Teachers Association, 1999).

On the specific topic of seeds and plants, parents may encourage children to explore their backyards or a neighboring lot or field for seeds, leaves, and other plant growth. Children may also make collections that would serve as the basis of a minimuseum (see tear-out sheets). Teachers may also create science bags or backpacks to take home with simple experiments or suggestions for cooking experiences.

The U.S. Department of Education has published a book for parents by Nancy Paulu, *Helping Your Child Learn Science*. This small parent-friendly volume is full of simple activities that parents can do with their children to enhance experiences with science. It is based on a hands-on, discovery approach.

◇ Evaluating and Assessing Children's Learning

Assessing children's concepts of growth and change in living things—seeds and plants—will be a continuous activity done on an individual and group basis using

- observations
- small and large group discussions with students as they work individually and in groups
- structured interviews with students
- portfolios of children's work
- children's self-evaluations and dictated stories about plant life

"Involving students in the assessment process does not diminish the responsibilities of the teacher—it increases them. It requires teachers to help students develop skills in self-reflection . . ." (National Academy of Sciences, p. 10). The tear-out sheets on pages 61–62 at the end of this experience can be used at different times during the school year to chart growth in children's knowledge of science concepts, and to help you plan your curriculum on the basis of children's current understanding.

-------------------------------------- **FOR THE CHILDREN** --------------------------------------

1. *Using Process Skills with Seeds*

Children are attracted to all types of seeds. After a nature walk, what teacher or parent has not found a child's pocket stuffed with seeds that they wish to keep as prized possessions? Teachers will want to be sure that the seeds children collect are not poisonous. Children enjoy the endless variety of shapes and colors and use seeds naturally to decorate their mud and sand creations as well as indoor art projects. Use their active experiences with seeds to build more formal concepts about plant life. Children should keep a simple science journal in which to record all of their active experiences with science.

Start with simple activities with younger children:

◆   Observe seeds and classify them according to size, shape, and color. Remember that younger children may be able to classify by only one attribute. Provide children with magnifying glasses to use while they examine the seeds. Allow children to feel them for hardness.

◆   Notice likenesses and differences in seeds. For this activity, provide the children with several containers of different types of seeds—vegetable, fruit, and dried bean. Talk about how they are alike and different. Allow the children to take some seeds from each container and classify them. Some children will use color, some size, and some shape. If they cannot find a basis upon which to classify a seed, encourage them to figure out another category. Children may add seeds from snacks, from nature walks, and from home to the seed project.

2. *Using Process Skills with Seeds and Plants*

After experimenting with seeds of all types, children will be ready to begin to understand how plants grow from seeds and how living things grow and change. Teachers may want to begin using simple scientific terms at this point.

◆   Encourage children to open beans or corn seeds that have been soaked overnight to discover the baby plant or *embryo*. Using questioning techniques, ask children what they see inside the bean seed and what it looks like. Provide materials for children to discover whether the embryo will grow without the rest of the bean seed and which seeds, when soaked in water, will yield baby plants. Children may wish to draw pictures of the small baby plants and dictate stories about them.

◆   Watch to see if children will suggest planting seeds. Children can watch seeds sprouting by placing them on wet sponges. One class of 4-year-olds walked through the seeds outdoors with wet socks. The socks were then put on a large table outside to see which seeds would sprout on socks in outdoor conditions.

◆   Plant seeds as a small group project with many choices for how children will undertake their own experiment. The teacher may want to have a discussion with the children first and chart the types of seeds that will be needed, how many, the type of soil, and the type of container. Children may want to decorate their containers to indicate the type of plant they predict will grow. Children will want to plant their own seeds. While there may be some failures, this will help children to explain what happened. In one class, the 3-year-olds learned that they could not forget to water their plants (even though the teacher, Ms. Gomez, had carefully put a small watering can next to the containers). The 4-year-olds in Mr. Green's class figured out that their seeds could not get air since they had been "buried." In most cases, it is important that children have success so that they will be able to describe what contributed to initial growth and how their plants grew and changed.

◆   Measure and chart change. Children may use measuring implements to see how tall their plants are growing. The several types of plants may be compared. Younger children may draw pictures to indicate the changes; older children may want to keep a record of the plants' growth over time.

◆   Keep a chart of new words learned and what elements were required to keep the plants alive. If the teacher allots time over the school year to the study of seeds and plants, it will be possible for children to observe the life cycle in action since children may raise beans, for example, and grow new plants from their bean seeds.

◆   Determine if children begin to understand the difference between "living" and "nonliving." Mr. Green put some marbles and rocks on a table with a few different types of seeds and plants. He asked the children to give him some ideas on how they could be classified. Then he made two columns and asked the children to classify on the basis of "living" and "nonliving."

◆   Build a terrarium. Help children to create the conditions that will keep plants alive. You may want to include insects that children have captured on the way to school or at home. Children may observe and draw or chart their observations at various times of day or over the period of a week or a month.

◆   Build minimuseums to house seeds and plants that are alive or have been dried. This is an excellent project to undertake with parents (see letter to parents on p. 59 at the end of this experience). Have a show at school to exhibit them to children, families, and the community. As part of the program, invite parents to eat foods that have been created using the seeds and plants.

3.   *Using Children's Books to Motivate Active Experiences with Seeds and Plants*

◆   Read *Dandelion Adventures* by L. Patricia Kite. Since the humble dandelion flowers almost anywhere, young children who live in urban environments will be especially interested in the journey of seven dandelion seed parachutes sailing through the air. Each lands in a different place: garden, sidewalk crack, park, school yard, woodland, stream, and a faraway land. Most of the seeds produce new plants with a yellow flower that is pollinated by bees and produces new seed parachutes. The book ends with several pages of facts about dandelions. Have children find dandelions outside. Look for the seed parachutes and try to see where they land. Draw pictures or do a group book on the life cycle of the dandelion.

◆   *The Berenstain Bears Grow-It: Mother Nature Has Such a Green Thumb* by Stan Berenstain will introduce children to simple plant science. There are simple instructions for planting seeds, cuttings, and tubers.

◆   Eric Carle's *The Tiny Seed* is another beautiful book that traces the growth of a seed to a flower.

◆   Read Nancy Carlstrom's *Wild Wild Sunflower Child Anna* and take the children on a field trip right into a meadow like the one Anna, a small African-American girl, enjoys as she talks to the flowers, whispers to the seeds, sifts soil through her fingers, and picks a yellow daisy. If there is no meadow available, try a park, an arboretum, or a green house; or like Tina in *Sunflowers for Tina* by Anne Baldwin, go on a sidewalk walk and discover a wonderful sunflower that has somehow sprung up on a nearby vacant lot. Be sure to take a camera on field experiences to record the children's discoveries.

◆ D. Florian's book *Vegetable Garden* helps young children learn how to harvest a vegetable garden. After the harvest, vegetables may be washed and eaten raw, cooked, or made into soup. Children can watch the transformation as they cook.

4. *Using Arts and Crafts to Document Children's Active Experiences with Seeds and Plants*

Plants and seeds lend themselves to beautiful artwork.

◆ As children explore in the play yard or park, encourage them to look carefully at the shape of leaves or the texture of bark. While young children will not remember the names of the different trees that they see, they can compare and contrast the leaf shapes. Take paper so that children can make leaf or bark rubbings that they can share with other children. Make a chart comparing the shapes and textures. Exhibit the beautiful rubbings.

◆ Children may also make leaf prints from the leaves they have collected from the ground, or iron (with your help) a leaf or an arrangement of leaves and seeds between two pieces of waxed paper.

◆ Create a root holder to view what goes on under the soil when the first roots of a baby plant are bursting out of the seed. See tear-out sheet 6 on p. 63 for instructions on making a root viewer.

◆ Make seed castings by pressing dried pods and other seed heads with interesting shapes into flattened pieces of clay in any shape. The seed heads will probably fall out eventually, but you will be left with a lovely impression in the clay.

◇ **Reflecting**

Ask children to organize their experiences. Provide them with exhibit space so that they can display their collections, plants, and the minimuseums they have created with their parents. Provide poster paper for children to dictate explanations and directions to be hung above their work. Additionally, make sure that children's science journals are up to date, illustrated, and displayed next to their experiments with plants and seeds.

Have a party! Invite family members and the school community to view the results of active science experiences. With the children, cook food that is made from plants and seeds. Have them observe how the ingredients change in the process of cooking. Serve the food to guests at your science party. (See the tear-out sheet on p. 60 at the end of this experience.)

◇ **Extending and Expanding to the Early Primary Grades**

Children in the primary grades can do the following:

◆ Expand their seed collections and sort them on the basis of more than one attribute, putting all the gray hard seeds in one container and the soft green seeds in another.

◆ Understand the process of photosynthesis: the concept that plants are the only things on earth that turn sunlight into food. Plants need sunlight, air, and water to remain healthy. Try these experiments from *Helping Your Child Learn Science* from the U.S. Department of Education.

- Have children look in a plant-care book, or ask an adult, to find out how much water each plant needs. Some may need to be watered more than others.

- Next, have them take two clippings from one plant. Put one in a glass of water. Put the other one in a glass with no water. Check each day to see how long the one without water can survive.

- Have the children observe and record what happens when a plant (or part of a plant) doesn't get any light. How long does it take for the plant to react? How long does it take for the plant to return to normal in the light?

◆ Ask better and more specific questions and make better predictions. They can also draw or record their conclusions in writing. For example, using the above experiments or others, have children make predictions about what will happen under different conditions before they observe and record.

◆ Collect and preserve plant specimens with the help of an adult who knows which are poisonous and which are rare and not to be collected. Children can make an herbarium by mounting pressed plants and recording the name of each plant they are able to identify.

◆ Understand habitats. Help the children to construct an insect terrarium. Some insects, such as grasshoppers and crickets, may be kept in a terrarium with a gauze or screen top. Plants and animals that live together in similar habitats out-of-doors should be selected. Air and drainage are important. A bowl of water, with stones or a twig over it, completes the terrarium. Children may then make continuous observations and predictions about how the insects and plants will behave.

◆ Design their own simple experiments. Have children generate questions about plants, seeds, and insects. Then have them design an experiment that will answer their questions. With your assistance, they may consult reference books. For example, a child may want to know if ants eat the spilled food on the sidewalk on the spot or carry it back to their anthill. Find out the answer through active experimentation.

◆ Profit from a field trip to a "hands-on" science museum, and arboretum, or the laboratory of a university. Preview the site ahead of time and make sure that the personnel know how young children learn. Introduce the trip and ask the children to generate questions to be answered. Upon your return to the classroom, reflect upon the learnings and document them by making charts, posters, or books about the experience.

◆ Utilize computers to locate the Web sites of science museums, and other resources for children. Teachers will want to make sure that the sites are suitable.

◆ Build a larger vocabulary of scientific terms. These may be recorded in their science journals and posted by experiments for easy reference.

◇ **Documenting Children's Learning**

A web can document the concepts, learnings, skills, and attitudes that children develop through their active experiences with seeds and plants: living things that grow and change. The web may hang in the classroom as a reminder of the integrated learning that took place.

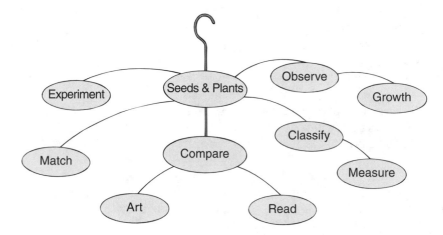

Date

Dear Parents:

As part of our science curriculum for this year, we are working on the theme "Living Things Grow and Change." We will begin with an examination of seeds and plants. There are many things that you can do to help us at school and at home. We would love to have you come and volunteer in the classroom whenever you can. Please let us know a bit ahead so we will be prepared for your visit. But if you can't fit a visit into school hours, please help us reinforce your children's scientific concepts.

When you go out, ask your children to observe what they see in the natural world. Let them tell you about it. Also, they may want to make collections of seeds and leaves to bring to school. We will be using them in several projects in the weeks ahead.

When children ask questions, sometimes it is easier to ignore them or answer with a word or two. Posing questions is really what science is all about, so we would really like it if you could take the time to answer your children's questions about nature and how things grow and change. **You don't have to be a scientist.** We aren't either. Some things you will know, and others you can look up with your child. We have a number of reference books on hand at school if you would like to borrow one. Either come in and tell us or send a note with your child, and we will send it home.

These are some places that you might like to visit on weekends if they are available to you: children's science museum, nature center, park, food store, and flower shop. At all of these places your children can find seeds and plants to observe. Often there will be someone there to talk to your children about their observations.

Your children will be keeping a science journal. Encourage them to illustrate their observations, and perhaps they can dictate sentences to you about seeds and plants.

Thank you for helping us with our new science unit. Your children are building the skills that they will need for the study of science in future years.

Sincerely,

Date

Dear Parents:

In the next few days, we will be sending a small backpack home with your children with suggestions for things that they can do at home to learn about science concepts. The experiences should be fun for everyone. They include things like planting seeds inside or out, making art creations with things that they have found in the yard or the park, and cooking with seeds and plants.

Each kit will contain simple directions. Don't worry if the projects aren't perfect. Children learn from making mistakes too. In fact, they will learn that plants need water if they forget to water them. This is an important concept.

There will also be directions for creating a minimuseum with your child. You will need a shoebox or other cardboard container, seeds, plants, dried flowers, glue, and art materials, or some of these items. We hope that you and your child can create something beautiful to bring to school.

Please let us know how your projects are going. Either call us, stop by, or send a note with your child. If you want to talk to us about a project, we will be glad to speak with you.

Please encourage your children to use their science journals to record their questions, the observations that they are making, and the results of the project. They will probably need help with the writing, but pictures help to documents science experiences too.

Thank you for taking the time to help us with science concepts. We hope that they are fun for you as well. We will be in touch with you in the next few weeks about a party and an exhibit we will be having to conclude Living Things Grow and Change: Seeds and Plants.

Sincerely,

Science Exhibit and Party
Everyone Come
Baby-Sitting and Food

Date

Dear Parents:

We are about to conclude our unit on growth and change in living things. We hope you have enjoyed the activities that you have done at home with your child. We greatly appreciate your help. Children learn so much from doing things with their parents.

Now it is time to have a party to recognize all of the hard work that you and your children have done in the area of science. We have all learned through your efforts. Your whole family is invited, and transportation will be provided for anyone who needs it. Just drop us a note.

On _____ at _____ in the _____ at school, we will be having a science party. The event will include the beautiful minimuseums that you have worked on with your children. In addition, experiments done at school, children's artwork with plants and seeds, posters listing the science words that we have learned, and other exhibits will be all around the room.

The children have been cooking with plants and seeds. They are surprised that some of the food is very familiar to them. Other things are new to some children such as toasted pumpkin seeds. We will have plenty of food on hand for all of us to sample (and more prepared by our wonderful cook).

We thank you again for working with us and look forward to seeing you at the party. Please come and bring the whole family.

Sincerely,

Group Observation—Science Terms

Date:

Center/Area:

Children's Names:

Science Terms Used (Record terms on the left)

	Accuracy		
	Not at All	**Some**	**Accurate**
1.	_____	_____	_____
2.	_____	_____	_____
3.	_____	_____	_____
4.	_____	_____	_____
5.	_____	_____	_____
6.	_____	_____	_____
7.	_____	_____	_____
8.	_____	_____	_____
9.	_____	_____	_____
10.	_____	_____	_____

Comments:

Date _____

Name _____

Age of Child _____

Individual Evaluation: Assessing Children's Science Skills
Living Things Grow and Change: Seeds and Plants

	Always	Sometimes	Never
Explores seeds and plants	_____	_____	_____
Identifies the processes that permit plants to live	_____	_____	_____
Observes a variety of seeds	_____	_____	_____
Compares a variety of seeds	_____	_____	_____
Classifies and measures a variety of seeds	_____	_____	_____
Observes a variety of plants	_____	_____	_____
Compares a variety of plants	_____	_____	_____
Classifies and measures a variety of plants	_____	_____	_____
Matches plants with the seeds they make	_____	_____	_____
Observes the growth of seeds into plants	_____	_____	_____
Observes how plants change as they grow	_____	_____	_____
Asks appropriate questions	_____	_____	_____
Reaches appropriate conclusions	_____	_____	_____
Uses appropriate terminology (age level)	_____	_____	_____
Can apply concepts from children's literature on growth and change	_____	_____	_____
Enjoys constructing simple experiments (with the help of a teacher or parent)	_____	_____	_____
Enjoys using plants and seeds in artwork	_____	_____	_____

Additional Comments:

Instructions for Making a Root Viewer

1. Take a 1-quart, square-bottomed plastic freezer container.

2. Cut from a top corner straight down to the middle of the bottom of the same side.

3. Make the same cut on the opposite side of the container.

4. Make a straight cut across the bottom.

5. Remove the cutout piece of plastic.

6. Using plastic tape, tape a piece of plexiglass to the open side of the container. Make sure there are no holes or gaps.

7. Tape a piece of black paper to the top edge of the plexiglass so that it can be lifted and lowered.

8. Place stones in the bottom of the container for drainage.

9. Add potting soil to fill.

10. Push a few seeds into the soil about one-half inch back from the plexiglass edge.

11. Flip the black paper down.

12. Water the seeds and place the container in a dark spot until the seeds sprout.

13. Then, place the container in the light and lift up the black paper every day to check on the roots.

2

Living Things Grow and Change:
Insects and Small Animals

─────────────── **FOR THE TEACHER** ───────────────

◇ **What You'll Need to Know**

Young children are highly interested in living things and are usually able to identify those they have an interest in or have had the opportunity to observe through books, films, or, best of all, directly. Most children of this age can describe the attributes of insects and small animals and distinguish one from another. They are familiar with bugs, although they may not know the proper terms to describe them. They have usually been exposed to fish, birds, some wildlife, and pets that live in their homes or in the classroom. It is wise to keep in mind, however, that some children are afraid of animals and will need more support in their explorations.

The teacher will want to provide opportunities for children, especially those who live in circumstances that limit their interaction with small animals, to observe a variety of animals in the classroom, on the school grounds, in the neighborhood, at home, in parks and gardens, and at the zoo. Yet, observing is not enough. As a teacher, you will want to encourage young children to ask questions for which they can find answers by looking carefully at small animals and then checking their observations with simple field guides and with one another. Young children need to experience science. As with seeds and plants, the key is an emphasis on the process skills of observing, classifying, comparing, predicting, and communicating findings. Gradually, through active experiences with small animals, children will build concepts that will enable them to understand the natural world and move toward concepts of human development. It will be necessary to confine experiences for young children to a few organisms since there are 200 million insects alone for every person.

◇ **Key Concepts**

- There are many kinds of animals.

- Some animals are alike in the way they look and in the things they do, and others are very different from each other.

- Animals need air, water, and food.

- Animals can survive only in environments in which their needs can be met.

- Many animals make shelters to rear their young.

- Stories sometimes give animals attributes they really do not have.

- Animals have life cycles that include being born, developing into adults, reproducing, and dying.

◇ **Goals and Objectives**

Children will observe small animals both outside and in the classroom.

Children will compare various insects and small animals and identify the similarities and differences.

Children will learn simple scientific terminology for animal parts and their functions.

Children will observe the life cycle of a small animal.

Children will identify environments where various small animals thrive.

Children will identify various shelters that small animals create for their young (nests).

Children will identify foods that are specific to different animals.

Children will identify stories in which animals are depicted with human attributes and feelings.

◇ **What You'll Need**

As with seeds and plants, you may want to consult the list "The Outstanding Science Trade Books for Children—1999" (books published in 1998). The following books, primarily for adults and older children, have resources on small animals:

1. *The Backyard Birdwatcher* by G. Harrison (Simon & Schuster). Contains many ideas for attracting and observing a variety of birds.

2. *How Birds Build Their Amazing Homes (Animal Architects)* by W. W. Robinson (Black Birch Marketing). Each chapter introduces a specific nest type (sewn, mound, clay) and the book has excellent photographs.

3. *National Audubon Society First Field Guide to Mammals* by J. Grassy and C. Keene (National Audubon Society). With the aid of the teacher, can be used with young children to verify observations.

4. *Insects (National Audubon Society First Field Guide* by C. Wilston (National Audubon Society). Use as above.

5. *Joyful Noise: Poems for Two Voices* by P. Fleischman (Harper Collins Juvenile Books). Contains poetry about the sounds of insects as they move and is to be read aloud by two persons.

6. *Animals in the Classroom* by D. Kramer (Addison-Wesley). Has good information on the correct handling of classroom animals.

7. *Creepy Crawlies and the Scientific Method* by S. Kneidel (Fulcrum Publishing). Is an excellent guide for the teacher on setting up experimental conditions for children's scientific observations.

Children's Books

Asch, F. (1999). *Baby bird's first nest.* San Diego, CA: Gulliver Books.

Carle, E. (1972). *The very hungry caterpillar.* London: Hamish Hamilton.

Carle, E. (1985). *The very busy spider.* New York: Philomel Books.

Carle, E. (1990). *The very quiet cricket.* New York: Philomel Books.

Dorros, A. (1988). *Ant cities (Let's read and find out).* New York: HarperTrophy.

Glaser, L. (1994). *Wonderful worms.* Brookfield, CT: Millbrook Press.

Herligman, D. (1996). *From caterpillar to butterfly (Let's read and find out).* New York: HarperTrophy.

Palotta, J. (1986). *The icky bug book.* Watertown, MA: Charlesbridge Publishing.

Parker, N. W., & Wright, J. R. (1987). *Bugs.* New York: Scholastic.

Rogers, F. (1988). *Mister Roger's first experience book: When a pet dies.* New York: Putnam.

Sandved, K. (1999). *The butterfly alphabet.* New York: Scholastic.

Scarborough, K. (1997). *Spider's nest (Watch it grow).* New York: Time Life.

Zakowski, C. (1997). *The insect book: A basic guide to the collection and care of common insects for young children.* Highland City, FL: Rainbow Books, Inc.

Other Things You'll Need

- Temporary cages for insects (see directions on p. 69)
- Plastic or metal cages for classroom animals if you chose to have them
- Live insects
- Preserved insects
- Hand lens and magnifying glasses
- Paper
- Crayons and markers
- Garden trowels and a digging place
- Dishpan
- Moist cornmeal or bread crumbs
- Large clean jars
- Fresh leaves
- Waxed paper
- Rubber bands
- Paper bags
- Notebooks or science journals for each child
- Sketch pad
- Net for catching insects
- Mounted pictures and photographs of various types of small animals
- Measuring tools
- Access to the out-of-doors as a laboratory

◇   **The Home-School Connection**

As with seeds and plants, questioning, listening, observing, and predicting work best when attempting to convey concepts about animals to young children. While often messy and time-consuming, the hands-on approach fosters concept learning. On the topic of small animals (insects), parents may encourage their children to search their homes and neighborhoods for bugs.

Some bugs are not "observer friendly," so parents should set clear guidelines for children on what to look for. Ants, almost all spiders, fleas, silverfish, moths, flies, and ladybugs are harmless. Parents can encourage children to observe how some insects such as ants work as a community. Children can watch ants around their anthills and observe how they "notify" other ants of food. In the process of observations, parents may pose questions and encourage children to dictate or write the answers in a science journal. Drawing pictures will assist children to remember their observations. *Helping Your Child Learn Science* by Nancy Paulu is a helpful book for parents.

◇ Evaluating and Assessing Children's Learning

Assessing children's concepts of insects and small animals will be a continuous process done on an individual and group basis using

- observations
- discussions with children as they work by themselves or in groups
- structured interviews with children
- portfolios of children's work
- examination of children's science journals
- children's self-evaluations of their interest level, their work, and dictated stories about animal life
- classification and matching games

The tear-out sheets on pages 76–77 at the end of this chapter can be used at different times in the school year to chart growth in children's knowledge of insects and small animals and to help you plan your curriculum to extend children's current understanding.

———————— FOR THE CHILDREN ————————

First, the teacher will want to introduce the topic of animals by arranging the classroom with books, posters, and animal exhibits. A discussion may follow in which children generate a list of animals based on the definition that "an animal is any living thing that is not a plant." Then a decision must be made by either the teacher or the children (with the teacher's guidance) about which animals to study.

1. *Observing Small Animals: Insects*

Children should have no difficulty locating creatures under rocks, on window frames, and on weeds. Catching them is more of a problem and should be done in small groups with care not to harm the insect. Open plastic jars, sandwich bags, and nets make good temporary places to house insects. Tongs may be used to capture and transfer them to a more permanent cage for observation. A simple temporary cage for small insects can be made by covering a plastic container with a piece of nylon hosiery, stretched and held in place with tape or a large rubber band. Respect for the environment is taught when the teacher asks children to release insects at the end of the day. One or two interesting insects may be preserved for displays.
    Start with simple activities.

◆ Suggest that they look for the things that identify an animal as a member of the insect family: three body parts, six legs, and two feelers.

◆ Encourage children to draw pictures of the insect they are observing and dictate a story or label insect parts.

- ◆ Encourage the use of proper terminology by using words such as *thorax* and *antennae*. These may be recorded on a chart as they come up in discussions.

- ◆ Compare and contrast insects by the way they look and the things they do. Have children make charts or a Venn diagram listing similarities and differences.

- ◆ Observe insects' social behavior. For example, fireflies may "light up" to attract mates.

- ◆ Observe how insects defend themselves. Some have coats of armor, and others sting, like bees and wasps.

Ms. Johnson, a teacher of 4-year-olds, posed this question to her class: "Is a spider an insect?" The children immediately responded that it was. She then asked them how they could be sure that they were right. They knew that they had to observe a spider and some of the insects they had collected. Small groups went to observe, recorded their conclusions, and shared them with the entire class. The answer: a spider is not an insect.

2. *Environments and Life Cycles*

Mealworms are easy to maintain in the classroom, and they may be purchased cheaply at pet stores, eliminating the problem of "catching." They must be put in plastic or glass containers since they can chew through cardboard and Styrofoam. They should be placed in bran and covered with a moist paper towel. Very little water is required since they are able to extract moisture from their food. Children may feed them small pieces of potato, apple, or broccoli. At this point, explain to the children that in order to grow healthy mealworm beetles, they need to create a growth environment or habitat just as the mealworm would do for itself.

- ◆ Have children take time to observe each day what is happening in the mealworm environment.

- ◆ Let students record observations in their journals with either descriptions or pictures.

- ◆ Have students watch as the life cycle replicates itself as the larvae seem to "die." Actually they are turning into a chrysalis stage. They will emerge from this as light-colored beetles about an inch long. They will mate and die in about a week. Their almost-invisible eggs will repeat the process, however. This is an easy way to observe the stages of metamorphosis, and the teacher may want to compare it to the caterpillar (see the list of children's books on pp. 67–68.) Have children measure and chart the changes that occur over time.

- ◆ Have children dictate new vocabulary words that emerge from their life-cycle observations.

3. *Nests*

Most children enjoy watching birds. One way to be sure to get a good look at birds is to set up a feeding station with a birdbath. Children can observe the various foods that birds eat such as sunflower seeds, chopped nuts, peanut butter, and fruit. By using birds as an example, teachers may set up experiences comparing foods that are specific to different animals: "How is bird food different from the food we feed our classroom fish?" Help children identify shelters that birds have created for the nurturing of their young.

◆ Have children try to spot a bird carrying grass or a twig in its beak and watch to see where it goes. Have children keep track of the nest over the season to see how the adult bird cares for its young.

◆ Start looking for active nests in the spring. Some birds nest under eaves and ledges and in other protected areas.

◆ Instruct the children to move slowly and quietly when they are near the nest since some nesting birds are easily disturbed by people.

◆ Use simple binoculars to observe birds at a safe distance.

◆ Start looking for abandoned nests to study in late fall. Ask children to identify the nest materials that were used by inspecting the surface of a nest.

◆ Have small groups of children take the nest apart bit by bit. Have them sort the materials into piles and see if there are any they recognize.

◆ Have children check their observations with field guides and simple charts.

◆ Use science journals to draw pictures or record observations.
   Note: In the United States it is against federal regulations to collect the nest of any migratory bird or endangered species. If you are in doubt, contact the U.S. Fish and Wildlife Service.

4. *Recognizing Children's Books in Which Animals Are Depicted with Human Attributes and Feelings*

Most of the children's books suggested earlier do not portray animals as people who talk and have feelings. You will want to make sure that children experience these books so that they will have an accurate view of animal science. You may want to read a book where wild animals are given names making them seem more like pets than part of the natural world. Sometimes motives are attributed to animals that make them seem human: " The fox wondered when the snow would melt so he could find food to eat." After reading the different types of books, ask children

• how the books are different

• which books seem to portray animals like the ones they have been studying

Teachers will also want to read stories in which animals have human roles, but it is important for children to understand that these are fantasy and that they could not really happen in the world as we know it. Children may not master this concept until they are in the middle primary grades, but it is essential to their understanding and respect for the animal world.

5. *Classroom Pets or Not*

Teachers need to examine their feelings about having pets reside in the classroom. Too often, classroom pets live under poor conditions. Children have not been instructed in the proper handling of them, nor is there a place for them to go on weekends and holidays. Davis (2001) tells of the near death of a beloved classroom pet when the Berkshire rat—Pork Chop—was dropped by a child. Pork Chop survived, but his cage mate, Curious George, "was unintentionally loved to death" (p. 85). These are poor messages to send to young children, both about death and about the dignity of life. In addition, if pets are to be a part of the science learning environment, children should observe and compare them, predict their behavior, test predictions, and communicate about them each day. Very often pets get stuck in the corner of the classroom and seem to have no observable educational value to the children. One solution is the "borrowed pet" who visits at intervals from the home of one of the children or from a wildlife facility or park. The teacher may want to prepare the children with questions about how the animal moves, gets its food, and protects itself.

◇ **Reflecting**

Ask children to organize their experiences. Provide them with space so they can display their artwork, journals, and charts. Also exhibit their predictions, observations, and conclusions about various questions. Have children exhibit examples of the foods that the animals they have studied eat. Provide poster paper for children to record differences in animal food preferences. If it is possible to display nesting materials, find an attractive space and add pictures and information on the type of bird, where it lives, and how it nurtures its young. Preserved insects may be added to the display.

Have a party! Invite family members and the school community to view the results of your active science experiences with small animals. (See tear-out sheet 2 on p. 75.) Surprise them with questions about small animals such as "Is a spider an insect?" Maybe the children will be the experts. You might also provide suggestions to parents for supporting the science curriculum as described in the preceding section.

◇ **Extending and Expanding to the Early Primary Grades**

Children in the primary grades can do the following:

- ◆ Make better predictions about small animals and ask better and more specific questions.

- ◆ Conduct more sophisticated experiments. For example, they can investigate the housing, food, and habits of earthworms by raising them in the classroom. Further, they can investigate how the earthworms affect the soil over time. Other studies might include raising caterpillars and hatching chickens.

- ◆ Use field guides to identify birds and wildlife.

- ◆ Utilize computers to locate the Web sites of science museums and other resources for children. Teachers will want to make sure that the sites are suitable.

- ◆ Build a larger vocabulary of scientific terms pertaining to small animals and draw and label simple insects. These terms may be recorded in their science journals and posted by experiments for easy reference.

- ◆ Investigate ponds. Many fascinating plants and animals live in, on, and around ponds. Visit a pond at different times of year to observe the changes.

◆ Classify and reclassify animals into more discrete groups. For example, instead of birds, insects, and animals that swim, children can form other categories such as where animals live, zoo animals, and endangered animals.

◆ Understand habitats. (See experience 1, "Living Things Grow and Change: Seeds and Plants".)

◆ Learn about animals that hibernate. L. D. Brimmer's book *Animals That Hibernate* has excellent photographs.

◇ **Documenting Children's Learning**

A web can document the concepts, learnings, skills, and attitudes that children develop during their active experiences with small animals. Teachers may want the children to take part in generating the learnings in the different categories. This will help with recall of experiences. Perhaps parents would wish to add to a general web or create their own web based on the things that they have learned about science with their children. The web (or webs) may hang in the classroom as a reminder of the integrated learning that took place.

Charts, diagrams, and exhibits of all kinds serve to document children's active experiences with insects and small animals. They should be placed around the classroom along with drawings and perhaps a bug mural (see the list of children's books on pp. 67–68). Teachers will want to encourage children to discuss their experiences.

Date

Dear Parents:

We hope you attended our science party based on the theme "Living Things Grow and Change: Seeds and Plants." Also, we hope that you have used our ideas to make collections of seeds and leaves, and gone out with your children to experience the natural environment or museums, nature centers, and parks. There are many things that you can do to help us at school and at home. We would love to have you come and volunteer in the classroom whenever you can. Please let us know a bit ahead so we will be prepared for your visit. But, if you can't fit a visit into school hours, there are many things that you can do at home to reinforce your children's scientific concepts. Learning occurs in many different forms and settings such as observing cloud shapes and naming things that can be seen, heard, or smelled in your neighborhood. The important thing is that you and your child are learning together.

Now we are studying "Living Things Grow and Change: Insects and Small Animals." We will be sending home some information about guess what—bugs! We know that some of them are real pests, but you and your child can learn from them. You will need an insect guide from the library (one with pictures is best), a magnifying glass, and your child's science journal. We have extra guides (also translated into Spanish) that you may borrow. These are the steps you might follow:

1. Search your home and neighborhood for bugs. They may be anywhere. Record where you find them with your child in the journal.
2. Try to identify the types of bugs you find using the guides. Record these in the journal and draw diagrams or pictures if you wish.
3. Identify the questions that you and your child have about the insects.
4. Write down the possible answers to the questions in your child's journal or just draw pictures of what you see to be analyzed later.

Thank you again for helping us with our new science unit on insects and small animals. Your children are building the skills and concepts they will need for the study of the life sciences in future years.

Sincerely,

Science Exhibit and Party
Everyone Come!
Baby-Sitting and Refreshments

Date

Dear Parents:

We are about to conclude our unit on growth and change in living things. In this period of study, we have focused on small animals. We hope that you have enjoyed the activities that you have done at home with your child. We greatly appreciate your help. Children learn so much from doing things with their parents.

Now it is time to have a party to recognize all of the hard work that you and your children have done with bugs and other small animals. We have all learned a great deal. Your whole family is invited, and transportation will be provided for anyone who needs it. Just drop us a note.

On _____ at _____ in the _____ at school, we will be having a science party. The event will include exhibits of all types including charts, drawings, experiments done at school (our famous mealworms), posters listing the science words that we have learned, our work with the identification of birds and nests, and observations of our "borrowed" pets.

There will be an exihibit on foods that birds eat, but we will also have plenty of food on hand prepared by our wonderful cook. We thank you again for working with us and look forward to seeing you at the party. Please come. It is important to your child.

Sincerely,

**Group Observation—Science Terms
(These terms relate to small animals, not plants and seeds.)**

Date:

Center/Outside:

Children's Names:

Science Terms Used (Record terms on the left)

	Accuracy		
	Not at All	**Some**	**Accurate**
1.	_____	_____	_____
2.	_____	_____	_____
3.	_____	_____	_____
4.	_____	_____	_____
5.	_____	_____	_____
6.	_____	_____	_____
7.	_____	_____	_____
8.	_____	_____	_____
9.	_____	_____	_____
10.	_____	_____	_____

Comments:

Date _____

Name _____

Age of Child _____

Individual Evaluation: Assessing Children's Science Skills
Living Things Grow and Change: Small Animals

	Always	Sometimes	Never
Observes small animals outside and in the classroom	_____	_____	_____
Compares small animals	_____	_____	_____
Identifies similarities and differences	_____	_____	_____
Learns scientific terminology for animal parts and functions	_____	_____	_____
Observes and records the life cycle of a small animal	_____	_____	_____
Identifies environments where small animals thrive	_____	_____	_____
Identifies various shelters small animals make for their young	_____	_____	_____
Identifies foods specific to different animals	_____	_____	_____
Identifies stories that depict animals accurately	_____	_____	_____
Classifies small animals	_____	_____	_____
Asks appropriate questions	_____	_____	_____
Reaches appropriate conclusions	_____	_____	_____
Constructs simple experiments (with or without help)	_____	_____	_____
Uses field guides and reference books	_____	_____	_____
Uses science journal regularly	_____	_____	_____
Draws and labels the parts of small animals	_____	_____	_____
Exhibits appropriate respect for small animals	_____	_____	_____

Additional Comments:

EXPERIENCE

3

I Am a Scientist

—————————————— **FOR THE TEACHER** ——————————————

◇ **What You'll Need to Know**

Digging in the sand, pouring water from one container to another, watching a spider climb the classroom wall—children use all the skills of a scientist. Children *observe* their physical and biological world: "Oh, oh, there's a spider," says Roberta. "I can count its legs—one, two, four," she continues. They *ask questions:* "Where does the spider live?" "Where will it go?" "Why does it have eight legs?"

With the teacher, they *plan* and *conduct investigations:* "Let's get a book about insects," suggests Danny. "Then we can find out where spiders live." Later, after looking through the book, Danny says, "There's no spiders here. What's wrong here?" And so begins a long investigation into spiders as children collect data, listen to experts, research books, observe insects and spiders, and finally *reach conclusions:* "Spiders are not like insects. Insects have six legs; spiders have eight."

◇ **Key Concepts**

Recognizing that children are scientists, teachers plan to foster children's abilities to

- observe
- question
- plan and conduct investigations
- reach conclusions, organizing their thinking

◇ **Goals and Objectives**

Children will develop

  observation skills

  the ability to ask salient questions

  skills in planning and conducting investigations

  the ability to reflect on their experiences and reach conclusions

◇ **What You'll Need**

Science Kits

Using fanny packs or small backpacks, create a number of science kits for children's use. These kits, filled with science tools, can be available in the science area so children who want to study their world can take them outside, or use them to study something inside the room or school.

Stock each kit with

- a magnifying glass wrapped in soft cloth
- small plastic bags with twist ties to hold specimens or collections
- a tape measure
- small transparent boxes for collecting

- a small flashlight
- a small garden trowel or spoon for digging
- small pads of paper and markers
- pieces of yarn

Clipboards

Also have handy a number of clipboards with paper and markers. Plain newsprint is fine, or you could premark the paper (as shown here) to encourage children's data collections.

Scales

Supply a balance scale and a regular scale.

Other Resources

What Is the World Made of: All About Solids, Liquids, and Gasses (1998), by K. W. Zoehfeld and published by Harper Collins Juvenile, offers teachers numerous ideas for introducing children to the nature of the world they live in.

Doing What Scientists Do: Children Learn to Investigate Their World (1991) by E. Doris offers teachers of young children guides to the scientific method. Especially useful are the examples of questioning techniques and facilitating the expansion of children's science experiences.

◇ The Home-School Connection

Children should develop the habit of using the scientific method at home as well as in school.

- Have children take turns taking a science kit home with them. Along with the kit, send task cards.

Task cards explain how children are to use the kits at home. An example:

Task 1
- Sit at a table and eat a cracker. Now look at the tabletop. What do you see? Use the magnifying glass to look at cracker crumbs on the tabletop. What do you see? Are the crumbs smooth, round, or pointy? Draw the crumbs as you see them through the glass. Draw them again as they look without the glass.

- Sweep up half of the crumbs in your hand and drop them in a clear plastic cup half filled with water. Observe what happens and sketch the results.

- Take the remainder of the crumbs to a place outside your door. You could mark the place with a piece of yarn from the science kit. Observe what happens to the crumbs over the next two days. Sketch your observations.

Task 2
- Scientists collect data, so have children take turns taking a clipboard home with them so they can record interviews with their family, friends, and neighbors.
    The task might be to

  - find out how many people they know like cats or dogs

  - ask who has made angels in the snow

  - find out whether their friends like vanilla or chocolate ice cream

◇ **Evaluating and Assessing Children's Learning**

Take a walking field trip around the school to observe how many different kinds of plants you can find. As you walk, observe the children.

- What do they attend to as you walk along?

- How many questions are asked?

- What do they discuss?

To further evaluate children's growth in using scientific inquiry, observe when and how children use their science tool kits. Note when they are used, where, and how children used them. Are they doing more than just playing with the tools? Are they taking the leap into putting two or more ideas together to form generalizations?

———————————— **FOR THE CHILDREN** ————————————

1. *Learning to Observe*

◆ Begin by making "*I Spy*" tubes. Obtain enough toilet paper or paper towel tubes so you have several for each child. Show children how to use the tube as an "*I Spy*" tube. Play the game "*I Spy*." Look through your tube and say, "*I spy something red and blue with white stars. What do I spy with my tube?*" Have children use their tubes to find and name the thing you've spied. Once they get the idea of using a spy tube, ask children to lead the game.

◆ Children could decorate their spy tubes if they wish. On a table provide paper tubes, paste, scissors, scrap construction and other types of paper, fabric, string, and ribbon, and tell children they can decorate their spy tube if they wish during center time. Ask them to make one tube to keep at school and one to take home. Label the tubes with their names so each child can have a personal tube to use throughout the year. Children can keep the tubes in their cubbies or in their science backpacks.

◆ Now go outside and use the tubes. Ask children to spy a bird or a specific plant, or to look at leaves budding on trees. On another day children may spy

- something square, round, or triangular on the school building

- something of a specific color

- the door they use to go inside the building

- a window in their room

- another child

◆ Continue observing.

- Obtain large magnifying glasses. Show children how to use these to observe their world.

- Take plastic hoops outside or make circles out of yarn and place these on the ground. Children use their magnifying glasses to observe, name, and/or count everything inside the circle.

- Make a small circle on the ground with a loop of yarn. Have 5-year-olds dig up the dirt within the circle and then sift the dirt through a wire strainer. Examine what is left in the strainer and what falls through. You might find insects, insect eggs, leaves, small stones, sand, roots, or seeds.

2.   *Learning to Question*

"Why is the sky blue?" "Who made the sky?" "How do birds fly?" Children ask questions constantly. And often they really do not want or need an answer; they simply are talking. Still, with all the questioning children do, one might think they need no help in learning to ask questions. Yet children, as adults, need to be able to sense a problem, and learn to ask and answer questions.

◆ Make sure children have the psychological safety to feel free to question. Think about classes you have taken. When you feel insecure or think your question would sound silly to others, you won't ask it.

◆ Offer and provide knowledge for children to question. Sometimes you feel secure enough to ask a question but don't know enough to be able to frame or articulate the question.

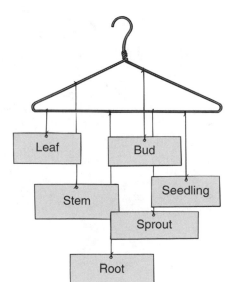

- Provide reference books on the topics children are studying or interested in.

- Seriously discuss topics with children. Research shows that teachers spend more time giving directions or correcting children than actually talking with them about what they are doing or trying to learn.

- Give children the vocabulary they need to ask questions. If you are studying butterflies, make a word hanger or chart with the words *chrysalis, cocoon, caterpillar,* and *butterfly;* if they are studying plants, the hanger might contain the words *leaf, bud, stem, sprout, seedling,* and so on.

◆ Teach children to pose questions. You might ask 3-year-olds to think about what they want to ask the police officer when she visits. Four- and five-year-olds can be asked to think about what they want to ask while on a field trip. List the questions on a chart. Then before going on the trip, cut the chart apart, and give each child, or teams of children, one of the questions. Read the question to them to refresh their memories. Then the children ask their questions on the trip. Take along pads of paper or clipboards so they can record the answers.

3. *Planning and Conducting Investigations*

◆ Young children, who live from minute to minute, have difficulty thinking about the future. Thus, making plans is difficult for them. Still, you can introduce children to planning investigations.

- Ask them what they will look for when they go on a nature walk around the block or what they think they will see.

- Have them make decisions about what they will take on the walk to collect things they find. They might elect to carry a plastic bag or a clear plastic box.

- Ask children to decide how many tool kits and clipboards to take along and who will be responsible for these.

◆ Conducting investigations involves a number of methodologies. You'll want children to learn to practice skills of measuring, categorizing, and organizing their observations.

- Measuring

  - Begin measuring with arbitrary measures. Children could find out how long and wide the sandbox is by walking the perimeter with their feet. Count and record the number of footsteps.

  - Walk different areas of the play yard to find out how big the yard or parts of the yard are. Again, count and record the number of footsteps.

  - Measure smaller things such as seeds, insects, or rocks. You might use small plastic blocks as the unit of measurement. Ask children to pick out the smallest, largest, widest, or thinnest insect.

  - Obtain a balance scale for children to use to find out which weighs the most:

    a large feather or a small marble

    a large empty box or a small unit block

    seashells

    acorns

    pine cones

  - Talk about children's measurements. Ask children to predict which item will weigh the most.

- Categorizing

  Children's natural need to find out and order the world in which they live leads them to categorize things in their world.

  Set the stage for categorizing:

- Make scrapbooks. Staple a couple of pages of paper between two sheets of construction paper and place the blank books in the writing area so children can use them as they wish. Once in a while, set up a table for making specific scrapbooks. As the younger children cannot handle magazines and at the same time cut out pictures, provide them with a bunch of precut pictures of animals, flowers, or whatever else you want children to categorize in their scrapbooks. Then they could make scrapbooks of

  Animals That Live in the Zoo, sorting zoo animals from precut pictures of farm, domestic, and other animals.

  Birds I See, choosing birds they have seen from a variety of pictures of birds

- Make categorizing trays. You could glue clear plastic boxes to a board. Then provide children with things to categorize such as

  seashells

  nuts and bolts

  buttons too big to stuff in noses or other places

  bells—cow, decorative, sleigh, or other types

  fabric, wallpaper, or tile squares to sort

  large marbles of all types to play with and maybe begin sorting by color or type

  plastic animals to categorize as farm, zoo, pet, or wild

  old greeting cards to play with and sort

◇ Documenting Children's Learning

Document children's learning by asking children to reflect on their experiences and organize their ideas.

Graphs

Using concrete objects such as small plastic blocks, large plastic paper clips, or other objects, children can document their findings through graphs, as shown in the examples.

What We Found

Seashells

Displays

Cover a tabletop with a cloth or brown paper for children to display what they found on their walk around the school. Make a sign describing what they did and found.

EXPERIENCE

4

How Toys Work

─────────────────── **FOR THE TEACHER** ───────────────────

◇ **What You'll Need to Know**

Children's natural curiosity and need to know drive them to want to know more about the physical world in which they live. By studying things in their physical world, finding out how things work, children's scientific skills of observing, questioning, planning and conducting investigations, and reaching conclusions continue to develop.

You might begin with children's toys, many of which use a source of energy. The source may be the children who move them up and down, on inclined planes or ramps, or up and over bumps and boards. Spring toys use the energy stored in the spring, which, when released, powers the toy. Electrical energy is stored in batteries, and the wind powers other toys.

Some toys make sounds. These sounds emanate from the vibrations of a part of the toy. Children can explore and feel these vibrations as they play with drums and other musical instruments.

Toys that are broken, or no longer in working order, can be used to find out how things work as well. After making certain all toys are safety proofed, and that adult supervision is constant, provide children with screw drivers, pliers, and other tools so they can take apart broken toys to find out how they work and perhaps, with assistance, fix them.

◇ **Key Concepts**

- Toys have a source of energy.

- This source may be the children themselves, or may stem from springs or electricity.

- Wind or air is the source of energy for other toys.

- Vibrations cause some toys to make sounds.

◇ **Goals and Objectives**

Children will observe how toys move.

Children will experiment by moving human-powered toys on inclined planes, ramps, and rough surfaces.

Children will compare sources of energy—human, spring, electrical, or wind.

Children will explore toys that make sounds through vibrations.

◇ **What You'll Need**

You'll need a variety of toys:

- wooden, plastic, or other toy cars, vehicles, dolls, and tops that require human power to be set into motion

- windup toys, such as cars, dolls, or other toys with springs

- toys that work with batteries

- wood planks for ramps

- drums and other musical instruments

- materials to make parachutes—cloth, string, a weight, and perhaps a washer

- materials to make pinwheels—dolls, heavy paper, and thumbtacks

- kites

- rhythm sticks

You'll also need an expert in electricity. This could be an older child or a teenager—someone who would work with the children with a flashlight bulb and bulb holder, some single-strand bell wire, and a battery.

Children's Books

The following books can be used to motivate children and integrate children's literature with science experiences.

Lionni, L. (1987). *Alexander and the wind-up mouse.* New York: Knopf.

Moss, L. (1995). *Zin, zin, zin! A violin.* New York: Simon & Schuster.

Pinkney, J. B. (1997). *Max found two sticks.* New York: Aladdin Paperbacks.

Rey, M. (1977). *Curious George flies a kite.* New York: Houghton-Mifflin.

◇ The Home-School Connection

Let parents know you are studying how toys work. Ask them to expand children's experiences by exploring how other things work at home. (See the tear-out sheet on p. 93.)

◇ Evaluating and Assessing Children's Learning

Conduct structured interviews with individual or small groups of children. Give them some toys that move by human, wind, electric, or spring power. Include a drum and rattle. Ask children which toys they like and start a discussion about how toys work. Let children play with the toys and talk about them.

Then ask them to do the following:

- Identify one toy that is powered by electricity, one by children, and another by wind. Ask children why they think each toy works.

- Play the drum and feel the vibrations. Ask children if they know any other toys or instruments that make sounds through vibrations. Record their answers.

—————————————— FOR THE CHILDREN ——————————————

Much of children's understanding of the energy sources that power their toys will stem from their incidental experiences. Think ahead about the teaching strategies you'll use to foster children's exploration of how their toys work.

1. *Sources of Energy*

◆ *Children as a Source of Energy:* As children play with cars, trains, or trucks they push themselves, provide them with two or more wood or plywood planks. Put a wedge under one plank to create a slanted road. Buttress this roadway with another plank. As children roll their cars and trucks down the plank, ask,

- How far did the truck/car roll?

- Could you make it go farther? How?

Then have the children roll one car along the floor and another car down the ramp, and ask,

- Which car rolls the farthest?

- Which car goes the fastest?

Next tie a piece of rope or heavy string to a few vehicles, and ask,

- Can you make the car roll up the plank?

Now have children pull them up the ramp.

While you're playing outside, take a few vehicles, planks, and rope with you. Have children try to roll their cars in sand, over the sidewalk, and through the grass. Ask them to compare and contrast their experiences.

- On what surface is it easier to pull or roll the cars?

- What causes the difference?

Have children record their experiences in sketches and drawings.

◆   *Springs as a Source of Energy:* You'll want to find a few vehicles that use springs as the source of energy. After children wind up the spring, ask them to repeat some of their experiences with cars they moved themselves.

- Have children wind up the vehicles and race them with those other children push. Ask children to measure which goes the farthest and the fastest.

- Try the spring-driven cars outside, on concrete, sand, gravel, and other surfaces. Compare the spring-driven cars with those pushed by hand over the same surfaces.

- Take apart one of the cars so children can see the spring. Have them watch the spring as they wind it and as it releases. Relate the spring to the motion of the car.

- Find other toys that use springs as an energy source. You might find a windup doll or animal.

- Read L. Lionni's *Alexander and the Wind-Up Mouse,* a magical story about a windup mouse.

◆   *Electricity as a Source of Energy:* With an expert in electricity to help you, ask children to experiment with lighting a flashlight bulb. Connecting the wires to the bulb holder and to the two points on the battery will light the bulb. Have several sets so a number of children can experiment at the same time.

- Find toy cars, other vehicles, dolls, or other battery-powered toys. Take these apart to show children the batteries. Four- and five-year-olds might be able to learn the − and + signs and to match these signs on the battery to those in the toy.

• Provide children with a few small flashlights. Show them how the batteries are inserted into the light to turn the bulb on.

◆ *Wind as a Source of Energy:* Young children have some difficulty understanding how the wind produces electrical power and other things, but they can experiment with catching the wind and observe the effects.

• Make a couple of parachutes to take outside. Take a piece of lightweight cloth or a piece of plastic bag about 12 inches square. Punch a small hole in the center of the cloth and in each corner. Tie a string to each corner of the cloth. Tie all four strings together near their free ends. Fasten a small weight — a metal washer — to the free ends of the string. Once outside, show the children how to fold the parachute by holding the center and rolling it toward the strings. Then wrap the strings around the cloth. Have the children toss the parachutes into the air as high as they can. After children find out what they can do with the parachutes, try some experiments:

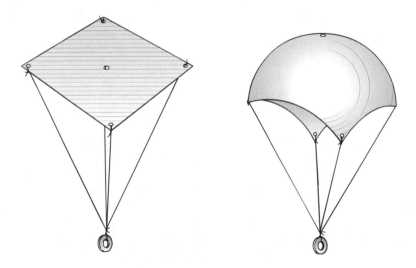

Who can toss the parachute the highest?

How far do parachutes fly?

How many times can they jump on both feet before a parachute hits the ground?

• Ask children to look at the parachutes and describe how one looks when it is first tossed in the air, when it fills with air, and when it falls to the ground. Back in the classroom, ask children to draw themselves tossing parachutes in the air (Seefeldt & Galper, 2000).

• Make or obtain pinwheels. You can make a pinwheel for each child by obtaining a 12″ doll, cutting and folding a piece of paper to form the wheel, and securely tacking it to the doll. Children haven't the muscle coordination to do this, but will enjoy playing with the pinwheels outside in the wind.

• Obtain a few kites and take turns flying these on a windy day. As you do so, talk about how the wind feels as it tugs the kite high in the sky.

• Read M. Rey's *Curious George Flies a Kite.*

2. *Vibrations*

A group of children's toys make sounds. The sounds are usually caused by vibrating, which in turn causes the air to vibrate. Observe toys that make sounds and try to discover the source of the sounds.

◆　Make rattles. Give each child two clear plastic glasses. Have them place a couple of sound makers (beads, seeds, pebbles) in the bottom of one glass. Help children tape the two glasses together to form a rattle.
　　As children watch the objects move and make sounds as they move in the rattle, ask children to speculate on what makes the sounds.

◆　Beat a drum. While doing so, ask children to lightly place their hands on the drum top so they can feel the vibrations.
　　Sprinkle some seeds on the top of the drum. As children beat the drum, the seeds will dance from the vibrations of the drumhead. Have them speculate on why the seeds move. You do not need to lecture or tell children what is happening; all you want is for them to observe and question.

◆　Invite an older student to play a string instrument for the children. Perhaps a student who plays a guitar or violin would volunteer. Ask the musician to show children how to vibrate the strings of the instrument to make sounds and to let children feel the instrument, and hence the vibrations, as they listen to the sounds produced.

◆　Read *Zin! Zin! Zin!: A Violin* by L. Moss. This book presents 10 musical instruments in a playful way.

◆　Read *Max Found Two Sticks* by J. B. Pinkney, the story of a boy who makes music by tapping two sticks on his thighs, the bottom of a bucket, and other things to make music. Have children model Max by making music with rhythm sticks. Remind them that sounds are made through vibrations and ask them to feel the vibrations of the sticks.

◇ Documenting Children's Learning

Make a group mural titled "*All About Toys.*" Divide the mural into four parts and label the parts:

Children

Springs

Electricity

Wind

Precut pictures of toys from magazines for children to paste under the appropriate category. Or ask children to draw their own pictures of different toys.

Date

Dear Parents:

At school we are studying how toys work. At home you can extend children's ideas of how things work by showing them how household items work. You might show your children how to change batteries in a flashlight or one of their toys and talk about the electricity that powers your tools.

Sincerely,

EXPERIENCE 5

The Earth: Water

---------------------------------- **FOR THE TEACHER** ----------------------------------

◇   **What You'll Need to Know**

Water and the water cycle are just a part of the physical setting that we call the earth. It takes years for children to acquire the knowledge they need to complete the picture since earth studies include temperature, states of matter, and chemical concentrations in addition to water. This experience concentrates on concepts of water, yet learnings relevant to other earth studies are integrated into the learning activities. Again, children will learn through observation, comparison, predictions, inferences, and the communication of conclusions. Gradually, through active experiences with water and its properties, children will form the foundation on which later abstract concepts about the earth can be built.

Since all living things require water to survive, our earth could not exist without it. Water is a readily available material that young children enjoy, and, as part of their study, they should be helped to learn that it is also a precious resource to be conserved. Children make discoveries through unorganized water play such as pouring, splashing, and running through the sprinkler in the summer. As with sand, clay, and blocks, children can use water without being constrained by the one right way to use it. Yet, when they are actively investigating a problem, they will engage in more sustained learning activity.

◇   **Key Concepts**

- Water can be liquid or solid and move back and forth between the two.

- If water is turned into ice and the ice is allowed to melt, the amount of water is the same as before freezing.

- Water left in an open container disappears, but water in a closed container does not.

- Water has weight.

- Water's weight and upthrust help things float.

- Water is a solvent for many materials.

- Water moves into other materials and may change their composition.

◇   **Goals and Objectives**

Children will observe and describe water in its various forms.

Children will feel, smell, and taste water.

Children will experience the weight of water.

Children will compare which objects will float and which will sink.

Children will observe air and moving air evaporating water.

Children will observe how changes in temperature transform water from liquid to solid and the reverse.

Children will discover which of a variety of materials dissolve in water.

Children will determine which materials absorb water.

Children will discuss the importance of water to life on earth.

Children will measure water using various containers.

Children will discuss the importance of conserving water.

◇   **What You'll Need**

Books for Adults

Agler, L. (1990). *Liquid explorations.* Berkeley, CA: Lawrence Hall of Science. Liquid properties organized for classroom use.

Butzow, C. M., & Butzow, J. W. *More science through children's literature: An integrated approach.* Englewood, CO: Teacher Ideas Press. Using children's literature to promote science concepts.

Crowder, J. N., & Cain, J. (1997). *Water matters* (Vol. 2). Arlington, VA: NSTA Press. Provides trips on the water highways and discusses water quality and how to protect it. Comes with six posters.

Crowder, J. N., & Cain, J. (1999). *Water matters* (Vol. 3). Arlington, VA: NSTA Press. A continuation of Vol. 2 with inquiry-based, hands-on ideas. Posters also come with this volume.

Diehn, G., & Krautwurst, T. (1994). *Science crafts for kids: 50 fantastic things to invent and create.* New York: Sterling Publishing Co. Some of these experiments may be difficult for younger children, but this is one of the new breed of science books that will immediately grab the child's attention with its excellent photographs and diagrams and its up-to-date language ("Wind Facts That'll Blow You Away"). It is also an excellent resource for the teacher.

Gartrell, J. E., Crowder, J., & Callister, J. C. (1992). *Earth: The water planet.* Arlington, VA: NSTA Press. Explains how water shapes our planet and daily lives.

Martin, D. J. (1996). *Elementary science methods: A constructivist approach.* Arlington, VA: NSTA Press. Over 150 inquiry-based activities for elementary students. Some may be modified for younger children.

Children's Books

Berger, M., & Berger, G. (1995). *Water, water everywhere: A book about the water cycle.* Nashville, TN: Hambleton-Hill Publishing.

Brandt, K. (1989). *What makes it rain.* Mahwah, NJ: Troll Communications.

Branley, F. M. (1997). *Down comes the rain* (Lets-read-and-find-out science, Stage 2). New York: HarperTrophy.

Hooper, M. (1998). *The drop in my drink.* New York: Viking Children's Books.

Jeunessa, G. (1990). *Water.* New York: Scholastic.

Marzollo, J. (1996). *I am water (Hello reader, Level 1).* New York: Scholastic.

Pledger, M. (1998). *By the seashore.* San Diego, CA: Advantage Publishers Group.

Relf, P. (1996). *The magic school bus wet all over: A book about the water cycle.* New York: Scholastic.

Weiss, E. (1999). *Bear Loves Water.* New York: Simon & Schuster Children's Books.

Wick, W. (1997). *A drop of water: A book of science and wonder.* New York: Scholastic Trade. Also a good teacher resource since it ends with a list of simple experiments.

Other Things You'll Need

- A transparent water table is preferable, although most are lined. A list of water play enhancers is endless, for example, soup ladles, strainers, funnels, measuring cups and spoons, squeeze bottles, corks, sponges, medicine droppers, detergent, colanders, strainers, and food coloring. Children may bring some of the items from home.

- Large, transparent plastic containers.

- Small, transparent plastic containers.

- Different types of paper, including paper towels.

- Styrofoam trays.

- Hammer.

- Large and small nails.

- Small wading pool if outdoor space permits.

- Large bucket.

- Plastic smocks.

- Access to a freezing compartment or freezing weather.

- Magnifying glasses.

- Assorted objects used to compare which objects will be supported by water and which will not.

◇ The Home-School Connection

There are many ways that parents can assist their children in developing concepts about water at home. Simply pointing out that moisture condenses on mirrors and windows at bath time, and that ice melts if left out of the freezer, helps in reinforcing school learnings. Snow and rain provide opportunities to discuss the qualities of water, how it feels on the skin, and what happens if you roll in the snow or splash in a puddle. Going to the swimming pool or beach, parents can encourage children to tell them how it feels to float or displace water by walking through it. Have children observe, predict, and test and record their conclusions. The teacher may want to send some ideas to parents as the unit on water progresses.

Some simple activities to do with children at home include making bubbles of beautiful shapes and colors. Just mix dishwashing liquid with water in a tray. Use a drinking straw and try out different-sized bubbles. What happens when a dry object touches them? Why? Encourage children to draw pictures or write in their science journals. Finally, teachers may suggest to parents that although their children should be free to examine the properties of water, water must be conserved since it is essential to life on earth.

Simple experiments to test what floats can also be carried out easily at home, even in the bathtub. Try a wood block, a plastic cap, one piece of aluminum foil tightly squeezed together and one spread like a boat. These experiments should reinforce the concept that things float when the weight is supported by more water. Bath time is also an excellent time to use different-sized containers, spoons, and cups. Children will soon learn that water and other liquids take the shape of whatever container they are in.

◇ **Evaluating and Assessing Children's Learning**

Assessing children's concepts of water and the water cycle will be a continuous process done on an individual and group basis using

- teacher observations

- individual and group discussions with children as they work by themselves or in groups

- structured interviews with children about the concept under study

- portfolios of children's work

- examination of children's science journals

- children's self-evaluations of their interest level, their work, and dictated stories about water

The tear-out sheets on pages 103–104 at the end of this experience can be used at different times in the school year to chart growth in children's knowledge of water and the water cycle and to help you plan your curriculum to extend and expand upon children's current understanding.

─────────────── **FOR THE CHILDREN** ───────────────

◇ **Indoor and Outdoor Activities**

The teacher will want to emphasize the theme of water throughout the classroom by using displays of children's books and reference books, posters, and photographs, and by using opportunities to experiment with water both inside and outside. Water play can be introduced by filling the water table. Children will gravitate to the table or container, which has been supplied with the many items described previously. To stimulate children's construction of knowledge, teachers may want to ask questions:

What does the water look like?

What color is the water?

What happens when you move your hands in the water?

Children should also drink water and be encouraged to discuss how it tastes. Children will vary in their answers, which will depend on their age and concept level.

◆ Display *A Drop of Water: A Book of Science and Wonder* by W. Wick, and read sections of it to small groups of children . The wonderful photographs will set the stage for children to view water as rainbows, bubbles, drops, steam, ice, and frost. Most impressive is a snowflake magnified 60 times its actual size. Next, teachers may want to arrange the classroom so that children can construct their concepts about water.

◆ As an outdoor activity, arrange various-sized containers around a small pool. Ask children if water can be heavy. Suggest that groups of children try holding different-sized containers filled with water. Children can chart how heavy the water feels (relatively) in different containers. They can draw pictures and record their findings in their science journals. The same objective may be achieved by using a water table inside, or having the children leave containers outside when it is raining and then try holding them.

◆   Have children compare which objects float and which sink in water. (Also suggested as a home activity.) Use dishpans of water and supply the assorted the objects listed earlier. Children may participate by bringing some of the items from home. The teacher may want to ask such questions as "Will the cork float?" Children will draw their conclusions and record them. Then they may want to try to see if the cork can stay on the bottom of the dishpan. Children can then classify objects as "Floaters" or "Sinkers." The teacher may want to assist children in charting their findings for display.

◆   Have children discover if shape plays a part in whether an object is a "Floater" or a "Sinker." See "The Home-School Connection" on p. 98 for suggested activities. This may also be done at school with dishpans of water and aluminum foil in two shapes (tightly hammered and spread out). Children's findings may be added to the chart and journals.

◆   Using assorted dry materials, help children to discover which will dissolve in water and which will not. Try salt, cornstarch, flour, salad oil, and sand. Suggest that children stir if they wish. Chart the findings under "Things That Dissolve in Water" and "Things That Do Not Dissolve in Water." Materials may be added as children become more sophisticated in their observations and conclusions.

◆   Depending on the location of the school, teachers can use resources to assist children in constructing the concept that changes in temperature transform water from liquid to solid and the reverse. Children can fill plastic bowls with water and put one bowl in the freezer and one in the room. Or, if the weather is below freezing, one container can be placed outside. Children should make predictions about the fate of the two bowls. Allow enough time and let the children compare the properties of the water.

◆   To prepare children for the concept that water moves into other materials on earth, ask them what will happen when they put water on different materials on their trays. Try tissues, paper towels, smooth paper, stones, and bits of fabric. Children can record their findings, which they will later generalize to geology. They may also conclude that water will flow faster or slower and in different directions depending on the material.

◆   To observe water life in ponds and streams, have the children make an underwater viewer. They will need the teacher's help with the cutting, but not with the observing that it makes possible. Using a plastic half-gallon milk or water container, carefully cut away the top, leaving the handle. Cut away the bottom of the container. Children may decorate it with water themes as they wish. Give children a piece of plastic wrap to stretch tightly over the bottom hole of the container, and hold it in place with a rubber band. To use the viewer, hold it by the handle and press it underwater so that the water comes up the sides but not into it. Peering down through the top, children will view slightly magnified creatures and plants.

◆ Read the short poem "Rain" by Robert Louis Stevenson. After the next rain, take magnifying glasses, science journals, and a marker outdoors to record the places where children find raindrops clinging. After returning to the classroom, have children generate a list of all the possible places that rain falls.

◆ Read *Down Comes the Rain* by F. Branley (illustrated by J. G. Hale). Have children draw or paint a picture and dictate a story about how falling rain makes them feel.

◇ Reflecting

Ask children to organize their experiences by providing them with a large area of the classroom where they can display their journals, charts, and explanations of experiments with water. The water table might serve as a focal point, with objects available to illustrate principles of water.

Have a party for family members to view and experiment with active science experiences involving water. Parents and siblings will enjoy comparing which objects float and which sink, for example. Children may create charts with simple directions for their guests to follow. Or they may pose questions such as "Which of these materials will dissolve in water?" They may provide sheets for family members to record their conclusions. Older children may exhibit a mural, drawings, or posters about our natural environment and the importance of conserving it. Serve food to guests at your science party with plenty of water to drink. (See tear-out sheet 3 on p. 105.)

◇ Extending and Expanding to the Early Primary Grades

Children in the early primary grades can do the following:

◆ Understand a water cycle simulation. You will need ice cubes, two metal trays (one for the ice cubes and one to catch the rain), and a heat source. Since the kettle or other source of water vapor will be very hot, the teacher will need to assist small groups of children with this project. Ask children what they think will happen when the water vapor hits the tray with ice cubes in it. Record their answers. Then hold the source of water vapor under or beside the tray with the ice cubes. Water droplets will be created on the outside of the tray. These droplets will fall down into the pan like rain. Have children write their conclusions in their science journals.

◆ Read *The Magic School Bus Wet All Over: A Book About the Water Cycle* by P. Relf and *Water, Water, Everywhere: A Book About the Water Cycle* by M. and G. Berger. Discuss the books with the children and have them draw and label their impressions of how the water cycle works. Discuss the importance of water for living things.

◆ Learn to love the earth and conserve its resources. Make frequent short trips outdoors into the natural environment. Model caring and respect for the natural environment. Explain that when too many waste materials are emptied into lakes, streams, and rivers, living things die or have less water. The children will be interested that no way has ever been discovered to make new water. Have them initiate an investigation into the ways water is cleaned in your area. A simple experiment in hand washing will show children how much water is wasted when they let it run. Just use a container to catch the extra water.

◆   Utilize computers to locate the Web sites of science museums and other resources for children. Teachers will want to make sure that the sites are suitable.

◆   Build a larger working vocabulary of scientific terms. These may be recorded in their science journals and posted by experiments for easy reference.

◆   Create a bulletin board on the thematic unit of water.

◇ **Documenting Children's Learning**

A web can document the concepts, learnings, skills, and attitudes that children develop through their active experiences with water. Teachers may want children to take part in generating the learnings in different categories of the web. This will help with recall of experiences. Perhaps parents would wish to add to a general web or create their own web based on the things they have learned about science with their children. The web or webs may hang in the classroom as a reminder of the integrated learning that took place. Start your web with "Water" in the middle. Then let participants generate "water words."

Older children may make a chart of the water cycle, beginning with "How Rain Forms." The teacher may further ask each child to find an interesting fact about water. These facts may be displayed as a mobile or illustrated on a bulletin board or mirror.

Date _____

Name _____

Age of Child _____

Individual Evaluation: Assessing Children's Science Skills
The Earth: Water

	Always	Sometimes	Never
Observes water in all of its forms	_____	_____	_____
Feels, smells, and tastes water	_____	_____	_____
Compares the weight of water in different containers	_____	_____	_____
Compares objects that float and sink	_____	_____	_____
Observes under what condition evaporation occurs	_____	_____	_____
Observes and describes how changes in temperature transform water from liquid to solid and the reverse	_____	_____	_____
Discovers which materials dissolve in water	_____	_____	_____
Determines which materials absorb water	_____	_____	_____
Discusses the importance of water to life on earth	_____	_____	_____
Discovers how much water is wasted in the classroom	_____	_____	_____
Visits ponds and rivers and observes water life	_____	_____	_____
Reads books about water	_____	_____	_____
Consults reference books about water	_____	_____	_____
Writes stories about water	_____	_____	_____
Helps in cooperative projects about water, including the bulletin board	_____	_____	_____
Asks appropriate questions	_____	_____	_____

Additional Comments:

Group Observation—Science Terms
(These terms relate to water and the water cycle.)

Date:

Center/Outside:

Children's Names:

Science Terms Used (Record terms on the left)

	Accuracy		
	Not at All	**Some**	**Accurate**
1.	_____	_____	_____
2.	_____	_____	_____
3.	_____	_____	_____
4.	_____	_____	_____
5.	_____	_____	_____
6.	_____	_____	_____
7.	_____	_____	_____
8.	_____	_____	_____
9.	_____	_____	_____
10.	_____	_____	_____

Comments:

Science Exhibit and Party
Everyone Come!
Baby-Sitting and Refreshments

Date

Dear Parents:

We are about to conclude our thematic unit on "The Earth: Water." During this period, we have focused on the importance of water to living things and conserving water. We have conducted many experiments, both inside and outside, to learn about the properties of water, where it goes, and what it can do. We hope that you have enjoyed the activities that you have done at home with your child to learn more about water. We appreciate your help so much. Children learn more from doing things with caring adults.

Now it is time to have a party to recognize all of the fun and hard work that we have had learning about water. Your whole family is invited, and transportation will be provided for anyone who needs it. Just drop us a note.

On _____ at _____ in the _____ at school, we will be having a science party. The event will include exhibits of all types, including a bulletin board created by the children, charts, drawings, stories, experiments done at school, posters listing the new science words we have learned, and experiments for you to do with your family. The children have posed questions for you to find the answers to. It should be a lot of fun.

There will be plenty of food for us to enjoy (and water to wash it down). We thank you again for working with us and look forward to seeing you at the party.

Sincerely,

The Earth: Rocks and Minerals

─────────────── **FOR THE TEACHER** ───────────────

◇ **What You'll Need to Know**

Through their explorations, young children are aware that the earth's surface is composed of rocks and various types of soil. By carefully observing and describing the properties of many rocks, children will begin to see that some rocks are made of a single substance, but most are made of several substances. The substances can be identified as minerals; however, the origin of rocks and minerals has little meaning to young children and should be left to the later elementary years.

School yards, backyards, playgrounds, vacant lots, and parks are good study sites to observe a variety of materials that make up the earth. As children collect rocks, they will become aware that soil varies from place to place in color, texture, and reaction to water. It is a good idea to revisit sites often so children will gain an understanding that the earth's surface is constantly changing. They can also simulate some changes, such as erosion in a small tray of soil in or outside the classroom.

Earth science is not about memorizing words and facts. It is about investigating familiar objects to build a foundation for future learning. Learning about rocks and minerals will allow many opportunities to compare, classify, predict, test hypotheses, and communicate.

◇ **Key Concepts**

• Chunks of rocks come in many sizes and shapes, from boulders to grains of sand and even smaller.

• Rocks are composed of minerals, but the amounts of mineral will vary from rock to rock.

• Rocks change by wearing away.

• Plants and animals left prints in rocks a long time ago.

• When rocks wear away and are combined with other materials, they produce soil.

• Minerals form crystals.

◇ **Goals and Objectives**

Children will observe and describe various types of rocks.

Children will describe rocks under various conditions.

Children will test the hardness of rocks.

Children will classify rocks by various attributes (size, shape, alike/different, color, smooth/jagged, hard/soft).

Children will observe the process of making soil.

Children will observe real fossils.

Children will make fossil prints.

Children will observe crystals.

Children will participate in making crystals.

Children will create art using pebbles/rocks, sand, and chalk.

Children will draw, label, and record their observations about rocks and minerals.

Children will learn new scientific terminology related to rocks and minerals.

◇ What You'll Need

Unless you are an avid rock hound, you will probably want to consult some reference books and have them available to you and the children as you plan your active experiences with rocks and minerals. Most of the following books for adults and older children have been recommended by the National Science Teachers Association or may be found in *Science Books and Films* published by the American Association for the Advancement of Science:

1. *Problems as Possibilities: Problem-Based Learning* by L. Torp and S. Sage (National Science Teachers Association). Offers suggestions for posing problems. Each phase of problem solving is mapped out so teachers know what they should do and what to expect of children.

2. *Explore Your World: Rocks and Minerals* by the National Science Teachers Association. Incorporates the Discovery Channel's acclaimed visuals, with more than 300 full-color photographs and visuals of rocks and minerals.

3. *Simon and Schuster's Guide to Rocks and Minerals* by M. Prinz et al. (Simon & Schuster).

4. *Earth at Hand: A Collection of Articles from NSTA Journals* edited by J. C. Callister and S. Stroud (National Science Teachers Association). Presents classroom strategies for older children, many of which can be adapted for use with students in kindergarten and the early elementary years.

5. *Rocks Tell Stories* by S. Horenstein (Houghton Mifflin). Points out that chunks of rocks come in many sizes and shapes from boulders to small grains of sand. Another book for older children that is good background preparation for teachers.

6. *Rocks and Minerals* by C. Pellant (Dorling Kindersley). Makes it possible to identify any rock. The eyewitness descriptions tend to be technical.

7. *The Best Book of Fossils, Rocks, and Minerals* by C. Pellant (Larousse Kingfisher Chambers). Treats the topic of fossil rocks.

Children's Books

Aliki. (1990). *Fossils tell of long ago.* New York: New York: HarperCollins.

Baylor, B. (1987). *Everybody needs a rock.* New York: Aladdin Books.

Christian, P. (2000). *If you find a rock.* San Diego, CA: Harcourt Brace.

Kittinger, J. S. (1997). *A look at rocks: From coal to kimberlite.* Danbury, CT: Franklin Watts, Inc.

Lionni, L. (1995). *On my beach there are many pebbles.* New York: Mulberry Books.

Marzollo, J. (1998). *I am a rock (Hello reader, Level 1).* New York: Cartwheel Books/Scholastic.

Parker, S. (1997). *Eyewitness explorers: Rocks and minerals.* New York: D. K. Publishing.

Rook, D., Coenraads, R. R., & Busbey, A. B. (2000). *Rocks and fossils.* New York: Time Life Education.

Stotsky, S. (1998). *Geology: The active earth (Ranger Rick's naturescope).* Broomall, PA: Chelsea House.

Other Things You'll Need

- Rocks of all types. You may need to purchase or "beg" rocks of various sizes in bulk from building suppliers or landscapers.

- Containers of various types for storing, observing, and classifying rocks. Egg cartons and muffin tins are good for small collections.

- Charts and posters depicting rock formation.

- Magnifiers.

- Hammers.

- Safety goggles.

- Different types of salts (table, Epsom).

- Newspapers.

- Sieve.

- Empty cans.

- Trowel.

- Water.

- Clay.

- Glue.

- Food coloring.

- Scales.

- Examples of minerals and fossils.

◇ The Home-School Connection

There are many ways parents can assist their children in the development of concepts about rocks and minerals. Simply observing and collecting different rocks on a walk to the store or during playtime in the backyard will begin the process. If families live near a beach or a stream, they may not only collect rocks of different sizes and types, but also have their children experience how the rocks feel when they walk on them. Both dry and wet rocks may hurt the feet, but wet rocks are slippery. How do the rocks look when they are dry and wet?

Children love rocks and minerals and tend to collect them in pants and jacket pockets without suggestions from teachers and family members. Family members can supply simple containers to begin rock and mineral collections. Then, they may suggest that children classify them in different containers according to various attributes, which will vary with the rocks that children found. Children may label the containers to indicate the basis of their classification.

Teachers may want to suggest that family members read the book *If You Find a Rock* by P. Christian. This book gives family members and children a variety of purposes for active learning experiences that are fun for all, for example, using stones for skipping across ponds, finding tiny creatures under them, and climbing larger rock formations. The book deals with emotions as well, so parents may want to suggest that their children pick a rock that reminds them of a person or place that they care about. After all, rocks provide stability to our environment.

Finally, teachers may want to send family members the instructions for various active experiments. In *Helping Your Child Learn Science,* published by the U.S. Department of Education, there is a suggestion for at-home activities involving crystals. Children may use magnifying glasses to look for crystals and inspect table salt, Epsom salt, a honey jar, and the walls of the freezer (if it is not the frost-free kind). Children will want to draw pictures of what they see in their science journals. They will want to inquire if all of the crystals look the same and if not, how they are different. It is not necessary for family members to spend a lot of time on rocks and minerals, however. Potential learning experiences present themselves every day.

◇ Evaluating and Assessing Children's Learning

Assessing children's concepts of rocks and minerals will be a continuous process done on an individual and group basis using

- teacher observations

- individual and group discussions with children as they work by themselves or in groups

- structured interviews with children about the concept under study

- portfolios of children's work (drawings, charts, labels, artwork, terminology, and stories)

- examination of children's science journals

- children's self-evaluations of their interest level, their work, and art and stories about rocks and minerals

The tear-out sheets on pages 116–117 at the end of this chapter can be used at different times in the school year to chart growth in children's knowledge of rocks and minerals.

---------------------------------- **FOR THE CHILDREN** ----------------------------------

◇ Indoor and Outdoor Activities

The teacher will want to emphasize the theme of rocks and minerals throughout the classroom using displays of children's books and reference books, posters, and photographs, and by using opportunities to experiment with the properties of rocks and minerals both indoors and outdoors. The sand and water tables are excellent places to experiment with rocks and minerals. Simple concepts of erosion are formed as children blow on sand or pour various weights of water into the same table.

The following activities should allow children to construct basic concepts of rocks and minerals. Make sure that child observations, predictions, classifications, and conclusions are recorded in science journals or charted for classroom reference. First, take children on a rock hunt. Provide them with containers to hold their favorite rocks. The play yard is a fine location for most rock hunts. More exotic rock forms will be found at a pebbly beach, by ponds and the banks of streams, and near large rock formations. You may need to be ready with examples of rocks that children will not find and your supplies from the landscaper. After the rocks are collected, you may implement various activities.

◆ Have children observe closely the rocks they have collected. Suggest that they use their senses—sight, touch, smell, and perhaps taste (if the rocks have been thoroughly washed)—to describe their observations. Provide children with magnifiers. After they have observed their rocks, have them share their descriptions. At this point they will begin to build their vocabulary of descriptive words such as *rough, slippery, pointy, round,* and the various colors. Make a chart with two columns. Ask children to tell you what they expected to see (column 1) and what they saw that they didn't expect (column 2).

◆ Suggest that children sort rocks that are alike in some way into the same container. Let children make decisions on how they will classify their rocks. Help them to record the categories that they have devised and suggest others based on the descriptive words that children use.

◆ While elementary-aged children can use the test for hardness suggested in Roma Gans book *Let's Go Rock Collecting,* teachers will want to use less dangerous materials for preschoolers and kindergartners. To determine which rocks are hard and which are soft, have children make scratch tests with their fingernails and with pennies. Rocks scratched by fingernails would be categorized as soft, the middle category would be rocks scratched by a penny, and the hardest rocks would resist a scratch by a penny. Have children create and decorate containers to house the rocks and help them to label the containers.

◆ Read L. Lionni's *On My Beach There Are Many Pebbles.* Using pebbles previously collected or bought, have children discover how the appearance of pebbles changes if they are wet or dry. Have children view them in the water table. Then they may remove some and check them the next day. Record children's explanations for the change in appearance. Show children how a drop of mineral oil or baby oil will transform washed and dried pebbles back to their original state. Children may use the colorful pebbles to make a centerpiece for their lunch table or to cover the soil in a flowerpot.

◆ Use rocks and pebbles and white glue to create a pebble sculpture. Representational or abstract, the form should be left to the children. Sometimes the shape or size of a rock or pebble will suggest a particular design. Do make sure children put their sculptures together before they use the glue so that (1) the design is pleasing to them and (2) it will sit solidly.

◆ Sand painting fits in well with activities centered on Native American culture. Have books with attractive photographs around the room. Using heavy paper, children will make a design with white glue. Suggest that they plan their design before they add the sand. Then sprinkle plain or different-colored sand on the paper and shake the excess onto newspaper. Older children may make more sophisticated designs by repeating the process until the paper is almost filled.

◆ Young children are familiar with chalk as an art medium, but they probably did not know that chalk is a rock. Children may draw with chalk on paper, old-fashioned "blackboards," and outside spaces where the rain will wash it away. Pencils are also rocks and can be examined for their properties.

◆ Children are fascinated with crystals and will enjoy making them with the help of the teacher. Dissolve salt crystals to make new ones. Dissolve 1 teaspoon of salt in 1 cup of water. Heat the mixture over a low flame to evaporate the water. The children will observe what is left. What shapes are these crystals?

◆ You may be lucky enough to find a fossil, but you will probably have to obtain one or take the children to a museum to see fossils. Explain that prints of animals, shells, and plants that lived on Earth millions of years ago can be found pressed between layers of rocks. These rocks are called fossils. Using clay, children will enjoy making similar prints of their hands, shells, or leaves.

◇ Reflecting

Children can organize their experiences by using a large area of the classroom to display their journals, charts, and artwork. Mini-imuseums can be created to house beautiful rocks and minerals. The teacher may want to organize small meetings of "scientists" to discuss what they have been exploring and investigating.

Have a party for family members to view and experiment with active science experiences involving rocks and minerals. Old and young will enjoy a variety of art activities and experiments that children have created as hands-on activities. Make sure the children provide simple directions to follow. Give everyone a chance to admire the beautiful exhibits (labeled) and the charts of new scientific vocabulary words. (See tear-out sheet 1 on p. 115.)

◇ Extending and Expanding to the Early Primary Grades

Children in the early primary grades can do the following:

◆ Form some concepts about the three types of rock formations. By collecting rocks and figuring out how they were made, they can get a glimpse of how our planet was formed. Teachers will want to have reference books, posters, and examples of each of the three categories of rock to use as they explain them and the children examine them.

1. *Igneous* means "fire." This was rock that was once melted liquid deep inside our planet. Some kinds of igneous rock came flying up out of the earth in volcanic eruptions. Others cooled and hardened before they made it all the way to the surface, but were exposed later by wind and rain. Granite, basalt, and obsidian are igneous rocks. Read *On the Spot: Volcanoes* by Angela Royston. This little informational book is full of visual effects and interesting details that children will love.

2. *Sedimentary* rocks started out as silt, sand, or smashed-up seashells floating in water. Eventually the tiny bits settled to the bottom, where they built up in thick layers. The weight squeezed the grains together, and minerals in the water

seeped into the spaces between the particles and bonded them into solid rock. Limestone and chalk are sedimentary rocks made from pulverized seashells. Have children draw with various types of chalk rocks on different papers to experiment with the effects. Ask them if they knew that the chalk they used every day was a rock. Have them use simple tools to smash sandstone. Ask them what they think sandstone is composed of.

3. *Metamorphic* rock is igneous or sedimentary rock that has been pressure-cooked under the earth's surface to form a different and tougher rock. Provide examples of limestone and marble. Marble is the rugged version of the "softer" limestone. Have children examine and chart the attributes of each of these rocks. Shale and slate may also be used to demonstrate the differences in metamorphic rocks.

◆ Read J. Marzollo's *I Am a Rock* and enter the Rock Hall of Fame where they will be provided with clues for identifying 12 rocks. (Labeled colored photos are at the end of the book.)

◆ Learn more complex classification systems for rocks and minerals.

◆ Build a larger and more complex scientific vocabulary pertaining to rocks and minerals.

◆ Work with more complex tools such as knives and hammers to open rocks and observe their properties.

◆ Work with machines such as those that polish pebbles to observe the results of motion on the pebbles.

◆ Access Web sites for information on rocks and minerals.

◆ Profit from a field experience to a science museum or the geology laboratory of a university. The teacher may want to preview the site in advance and have children generate the questions that they would like to have answered by the docent or student. More and more, docents are being trained to speak to children at their level, to answer their questions and introduce concepts that are not too advanced.

◇ **Documenting Children's Learning**

A web can document the concepts, learnings, skills, and attitudes that children have developed through their active experiences with rocks and minerals. Teachers will want the children to take part in generating various sections of the web. This will assist with reflections and recall. Parents might wish to add to a general web or create their own webs based on the things they have learned about science with their children. An activity at the party might be the creation of several webs to hang in the classroom as a reminder of the integrated learning that took place.

Child-made bulletin boards, minimuseums, word walls, Venn diagrams, and labeled displays all document children's new concepts of rocks and minerals.

Science Exhibit and Party
Everyone Come!
Baby-Sitting and Refreshments

Date

Dear Parents:

We are about to conclude our thematic unit on "The Earth: Rocks and Minerals." During this period, we have focused on the composition of the earth and the beauty and importance of various types of rocks and minerals. We have conducted many experiments, both indoors and outside, to investigate the properties of rocks, classify them, and see what happens to them under certain conditions. We hope that you have enjoyed the activities that you have done at home with your child to learn more about rocks and minerals, large and small. We also hope that you have enjoyed the books that we suggested. Please let us know if you have any book ideas for us. We are anxious to hear how your explorations with crystals turned out.

Now it is time to have a party to recognize all of the fun and hard work that we have had learning about rocks and minerals. Your whole family is invited, and transportation will be provided for anyone who needs it. Just drop us a note.

On _____ at _____ in the _____ at school, we will be having a science party. The event will include exhibits of all types, including your children's wonderful artwork with rocks and minerals. Rock drawings, posters listing the new science words we have learned, and experiments and art for you to do with your family will be featured.

There will be plenty of refreshments for us to enjoy. We thank you again for working with us and look forward to seeing you at the party.

Sincerely,

Group Observation—Science Terms
(These terms refer to rocks, minerals, and fossils.)

Date:

Center/Outside:

Children's Names:

Science Terms Used (Record terms on the left)

	Accuracy		
	Not at All	**Some**	**Accurate**
1.	_____	_____	_____
2.	_____	_____	_____
3.	_____	_____	_____
4.	_____	_____	_____
5.	_____	_____	_____
6.	_____	_____	_____
7.	_____	_____	_____
8.	_____	_____	_____
9.	_____	_____	_____
10.	_____	_____	_____

Comments:

Date _____

Name _____

Age of Child _____

Individual Evaluations: Assessing Children's Science Skills
The Earth: Rocks and Minerals

	Always	Sometimes	Never
Observes various types of rocks	_____	_____	_____
Describes rocks verbally and in science journal under various conditions	_____	_____	_____
Tests the hardness of rocks	_____	_____	_____
Classifies rocks by various attributes (complexity will vary with age/stage)	_____	_____	_____
Observes contents of soil	_____	_____	_____
Observes fossils	_____	_____	_____
Makes fossil prints	_____	_____	_____
Observes crystals	_____	_____	_____
Participates in making crystals	_____	_____	_____
Creates art using:			
Pebbles/rocks	_____	_____	_____
Sand	_____	_____	_____
Chalk	_____	_____	_____
Reads about rocks and minerals	_____	_____	_____
Consults reference books about rocks and minerals	_____	_____	_____
Writes stories about rocks and minerals	_____	_____	_____
Discusses rocks and minerals	_____	_____	_____
Asks appropriate questions	_____	_____	_____

Additional Comments:

Permission is granted by the publisher to reproduce this page.

117

The Human Body: The Senses

─────────────── **FOR THE TEACHER** ───────────────

◇ **What You'll Need to Know**

Children, as adults, use their five senses to find out about their surroundings and them-selves. When educators say that hands-on activities are best in facilitating children's learning, what they often mean is that children should be encouraged to use all of their senses to take in information and utilize it to answer the questions posed by their envi-ronment. Different senses provide different information for the child. Younger children are capable of understanding only one or two attributes of a thing such as an apple. When senses are coordinated, such as smelling and tasting, more information becomes available to form a concept of "apple." So older children should also be encouraged to understand how their senses work together. Through active experiences based on the senses, children may also gain an understanding of people who have impaired sensory abilities such as hearing and visual impairments.

◇ **Key Concepts**

- There are five senses—hearing, smell, taste, touch, and vision.

- All of the senses can be used to find out about people, places, and things.

- Used together, the senses can give us more information.

- It is necessary to practice using our senses so they will help us learn more efficiently.

- Some persons are not able to use one or more of their senses.

◇ **Goals and Objectives**

Children will name the five senses.

Children will be able to tell how each sense helps us learn.

Children will associate a part of the human body with each sense.

Children will use one or more of the five senses to discover properties of objects in the environment.

Children will compare objects using only one sense.

Children will classify objects using only one sense.

Children will describe how two or more senses work together.

Children will appreciate the senses as a learning tool.

Children will develop an understanding of persons with sensory impairments such as hearing or visual impairments.

◇ **What You'll Need**

You will want to consult some reference books and have them available to you and the children as you plan your active experiences with the senses. The following are recom-mended for adults and older children:

1. *The Science Book of the Senses* by N. Ardley (Harcourt Brace Jovanovich).

2. *Natural History of the Senses* by D. Ackerman (Vintage Books).

3. *Seeing, Smelling, and Hearing the World* by M. Pines (Howard Hughs Medical Institute).

4. *The Concise Encyclopedia of the Human Body* by D. Bumie (DK Publishing, Inc.).

5. *The Human Body* by J. Miller (Viking). A pop-up book illustrating the human body.

6. *Kids Discover: The Five Senses* by S. Sands (Kids Discover, 1(3)). This magazine explores each sense separately with diagrams and photographs. It discusses the need to use the senses to experience life.

The *Five Senses* books by M. Rius, J. M. Parramon, and J. J. Puig (Barron's Educational Series) explore sight, hearing, smell, touch, and taste. Most of them can be found in the original Spanish.

The teacher may also want to consult *Science & Children,* a journal written by and for teachers and published by the National Science Teachers Association.

Children's Books

Aliki (1990). *My five senses (Let's read and find out book).* New York: Harper Trophy.

Ballard, C. (1998). *How do we feel and touch? (How your body works).* Austin, TX: Raintree.

Ballard, C. (1998). *How do we taste and smell? (How your body works).* Austin, TX: Raintree.

Booth, B. (1991). *Mandy.* New York: Lothrop, Lee & Shepard.

Cromwell, S. (1998). *How do I know it's yucky?: And other questions about the senses (Body wise).* Des Plains, IL: Rigby Interactive.

Hewitt, S. (1999). *The five senses (It's science).* Danbury, CT: Children's Press.

Martin, B., Jr., & Carle, E. (1970). *Brown bear, brown bear, what do you see?* New York: Holt, Rinehart and Winston.

Martin, B., Jr., & Carle, E. (1997). *Polar bear, polar bear, what do you hear?* New York: Henry Holt & Co.

McMillan, B. (1994). *Sense suspense.* New York: Scholastic.

Oxenbury, H. (1985). *I hear, I see, I touch.* New York: Alfred A. Knopf, Inc.

Showers, P. (1990). *Ears are for hearing.* New York: Thomas Y. Crowell.

Showers, P. (1993). *The listening walk.* New York: Harper Trophy.

Walpole, B. (1997). See for yourself series: Touch smell and taste, seeing, and hearing. Austin, TX: Raintree.

Wood, N., & Rye, J. (1991). *Listen. . . What do you hear?* New York: Troll Associates.

Wood, N., & Willey, L. (1991). *Touch . . . What do you feel?* Mahwah, NJ: Troll Associates.

Other Things You'll Need

Materials and equipment for assisting children in learning about and appreciating their senses are endless. They will be listed in conjunction with each active learning experience described on the following pages.

◇ **The Home-School Connection**

The home and its environs offer many, many opportunities for parents and children to explore the senses and share sensory experiences. Both inside and outside, there are things to see, smell, hear, taste, and touch. When parents encourage close observation through the senses, children learn the importance of their perceptual functions in concept formation.

Parents (and teachers too) need to formulate safety rules for sensory exploration. For example, not all things should be tasted or touched. Children should taste and touch only those items that parents approve. Parents will probably be aware of their children's allergies, but teachers should certainly be informed. The senses also warn children about danger, but they may not be fully aware that a very hot burner in the kitchen will seriously burn them.

The following experiences require almost no preparation on the part of parents except perhaps time. Teachers may want to send these suggestions home through a handout or newsletter or discuss them at a meeting with parents.

- Parents can help children to sharpen their listening skills. Read P. Showers' *The Listening Walk.* After discussing the things that parents and children may hear on a walk (especially if they are quiet), parents may venture out with their children to take a walk. Parents and older children should record everything they can hear. These sounds vary with the time of day and the location of their home. For example, city children will probably hear cars, airplanes, buses, and the chatter of people and businesses. Children in the country may hear the wind, rustling leaves, small animals, birds, and insects. As a follow-up activity (or for a parent meeting or party), teachers may ask parents to assist children in recording their findings, then go back to class and compare the sounds that were heard. Did children hear the same things? Sounds may be charted with comparisons.

- As parents invite children to help with regular cooking routines or a special dinner, children may taste, smell, feel, and observe ingredients before, during, and after the cooking process. Parents and children may make a list of everything that was experienced by each of the senses. Of course, everyone gets to eat the food and to describe its texture. Making popcorn is a simple and inexpensive way for children to have a sensory experience. Making popcorn engages all of the senses. Children hear it pop, watch the transformation from corn to "puff," and smell the corn as it pops. Comparison can be made between the kernel and the finished product, between popcorn with and without salt.

Potential learning experiences for families based upon the senses present themselves every day. Teachers may want to remind parents to capitalize upon sensory experiences and heighten their awareness of the opportunities available. For example, "Taste this salt that I am adding to the stew and tell me about it."

◇ **Evaluating and Assessing Children's Learning**

Assessing children's understanding and appreciation of the five senses (and their combinations) for learning will be a continuous process done on an individual and group basis using

- teacher observations

- individual and group discussions with children as they work and think by themselves and in groups

- structured interviews with children about their sensory experiences

- portfolios of children's work (drawings, charts, labels, artwork, correct usage of terminology, stories, feedback from home)

- examination of children's science journals

- children's self-evaluations of their interest level and their participation in active experiences revolving around the senses

The tear-out sheets on pages 130–131 at the end of this experience can be used at different times in the school year to chart growth in children's knowledge of and appreciation of the senses as a learning tool.

FOR THE CHILDREN

The teacher will want to fill the classroom with books, charts, materials, and experiments that emphasize the five senses. Younger children are not ready to associate learning through the senses with "how" the senses work, but they can understand that they acquire much new information about their environment and the things and people in it as they taste, smell, touch, see, and listen. Children will also develop many new vocabulary words to describe their sensory experiences. These should be recorded in science journals or charted by the teacher for exhibit.

The outside environment is also a wonderful place to plan activities around the senses. Children will be able to describe clouds and bugs through close observation, listen to the wind blowing the leaves or the chirp of a cricket, feel the texture of tree bark, smell flowers, and even taste berries (with the teacher's approval). They will also learn to appreciate the beauty of the outdoors. Older children may develop some strategies to preserve it. City neighborhoods are filled with opportunities for sensory experiences as well. The smells of foods cooking, the sampling of a cookie from the neighborhood bakery, the sound of traffic, the textures of old buildings, and the sight of signs and posters can all be described and recorded.

Children may also be introduced to one or more categories of sensory impairment such as visual or hearing, and begin to understand what the impairment means for the person. They will also understand better how to assist a visually or hearing-impaired child in their inclusive classroom.

Begin by reading Aliki's *My Five Senses* as a general introduction. Make a big chart; divide it into five columns and label the columns with the five senses. Cut up some fruit and give each child a piece to explore. Ask the children to think of words that describe how the inside of the fruit looks, smells, feels, sounds, and tastes. Record the words on the chart. Bring in other objects for children to explore.

The following activities are clustered by the particular sense. Further activities for older children emphasize how the senses work together. All activities should be based on predictions, inquiry, and findings. Read B. McMillan's *Sense Suspense*. Have children guess which sense is depicted on a page. The answer will be on the following page.

1. *Sound*

◆ Noise! Noise! Noise! Make sound shakers out of plastic film containers, yogurt or cottage cheese cups, or other opaque plastic containers with lids. Fill the containers partially full of dry seeds, dry beans, rice, pebbles, sand, shredded paper, coins, and marbles. Make sure the containers are well sealed. There are several activities to do with these noisemakers. First, play a guessing game. Have children guess what is inside of the sound shaker by trying it out a number of times and describing the sound. Teachers can record the answers on a chart. Next, have children compare the sounds made by different materials. Which are different? Which sound pretty much the same? Finally, children can decorate the containers, label them, and make them a permanent part of the classroom to be used for singing, dance, and movement activities. Children will also have fun at the class party having their families guess what is in the containers.

Materials:

Plastic containers

Glue or tape

Fillings (dry seeds, uncooked beans, rice, sand, pebbles, marbles or coins)

◆   Play a tape or CD with different sound effects. Play each sound and see if small groups of children (listening closely) can determine what made it. Some recordings of classical music use instruments to imitate certain sounds in the environment. Have children guess what the instrument wants them to hear—sirens, the wind, a waterfall?

Materials:

Sound-effect recording or recording of classical music

Device for playing the recording

◆   Read *Mandy* by Barbara Booth. Ask children what they know about hearing impairments and hearing aids. Play a video without the sound and ask children why it was difficult to understand the video. Record children's perceptions of what it would be like to have a hearing loss. If possible, have a classroom visitor who is expert on hearing impairments to demonstrate ways to compensate for a hearing loss and how children can assist their hearing-impaired peers. Make sure your visitor knows how to speak with young children.

Materials:

The book *Mandy*

Video

Chart

Resource person

2. *Smell*

◆   Collect several items that have distinctive smells. Some examples are lemon, mint, pine needles, vanilla, vinegar, onion, and cedar wood. Keep the items enclosed in plastic containers so they do not mix. Either blindfold the children (some children are afraid of blindfolds) or punch holes in the lids and ask the children to do the following:

• Try to describe the odor and identify what is in the container. Record responses in journals or on chart paper.

• Rate the odor from good to bad. The rating may vary by child. Some people like smells that others avoid. Discuss why the smell is good or bad.

- Draw a picture about what the smell reminds them of. For example, vanilla may remind them of making cakes and cedar wood of camping. Have children dictate a story about their drawing.

  Materials:

  Items to smell

  Paper and writing implements for stories

  Blindfold or perforated container to hold "smelly" items

◆ Plan a walking trip outside of the classroom. The great outdoors is full of wonderful smells. Have children describe the smells and record them in the science journal or on chart paper. If you are in an area where there are different seasons, compare the smells of spring, summer, fall, and winter. An interesting "smelling trip" would include places around the school such as the kitchen or cafeteria, the main office, the bathrooms, and the library. Each has distinctive smells. Have children record the smells that they discover and compare them with the findings of other children.

  Materials:

  Science journals or chart paper

◆ Create "smell cards" for memory or matching type games. Children may collect and dry herbs or flowers that have a strong smell. Glue or tape the items to small pieces of cardboard.

  Materials:

  Things to smell such as dried herbs and flowers

  Paper

  Glue or tape

3. *Touch*

◆ Gather a number of things that are cold, hot, smooth, or rough such as sandpaper, ice, warm water, an apple. Work in small groups. Have children close their eyes and tell you what they feel when you touch the items to their hands or fingertips.

  Materials:

  Items to touch

◆ Have children bring items with different textures from home or from the outdoors to create a "Please Touch Me" tray. Items may be added and subtracted as children tire of them. Be sure to have the children record the item and their perception of its texture in their science journals. They may want to add drawings and written labels.

  Materials:

  Large tray

  Items for tray

  Science journals and pens or markers

◆ Get several grades of sandpaper from a hardware store. Cut them into pieces of the same size. Be sure to write the degree of roughness on the back of each piece. This is a self-correcting activity. Mix the pieces up, have the children put them in order, and then check if to see if they are right. If not, have them record where they made their mistake.

Materials:

Sandpaper of various degrees of roughness

Science journals and writing materials

Sweet	Bitter	Sour	Salty
✓			
			✓
		✓	
✓			
	✓		
	✓		

4. *Taste*

◆ *Make a chart with headings: Sweet, Bitter, Sour, Salty.* Gather several foods that fit into these four categories of taste. Cut them into small pieces. Have the children taste one at a time and vote on which category it fits into. If there is a disagreement, have the children state why they picked a category. Continue until all food items are categorized. Have children discuss which taste they prefer and why. Chart the results.

Materials:

Food items

Chart paper and marker

◆ Have the children decide on a cooking activity. Confine their choices to foods that require a few simple ingredients. All ingredients should be available for them to taste. Then do a taste test of the final product. Can they identify any of the individual ingredients? If so, which ones? How does the cooked product taste with all of the ingredients combined? Cakes or simple stews work well for this experience.

Materials:

Ingredients for a cooking activity of the children's choice

Cooking utensils, pots or pans

A small oven

Spoons for tasting

5. *Sight*

Children who are not visually impaired depend on sight for most of the information that they bring in through the senses unless they are continually reminded to use their other sensory apparatuses. Activities related to sight should be centered on developing an appreciation for information acquired visually and encouraging children to observe or look more closely at the things that they take for granted. Do things really look the way they appear at first glance? Every place you go with children, ask them to describe what they are seeing and encourage them to look more carefully. They may discover a small animal or bird that appears to be hidden unless they look very carefully.

◆ In a small group, have children attempt to describe an object while they are blindfolded or have their eyes closed. Young children will not close their eyes for long, but you can record their perceptions from touch, smell, and sound immediately.

Record the vocabulary words they use. Have children guess what the object is based on their sensory observations. Then, let them open their eyes and see if they were right. Ask children how they could assist a visually impaired classmate in "visualizing" an object such as a block shape, a car, or a doll. Have them draw a picture and dictate a story about what it would be like to be visually impaired.

◆ Set up a corner of the classroom with colored water, a prism, a microscope, and a magnifying glass. Younger children may need help with the microscope. Have them hold the prism to the light. What do they see? Observe closely. Help them to record as many words as they can to describe their observations. Have them observe the colored water with the magnifying glass, then with the microscope. These scientific tools can be used with small objects found outside or with pond water to magnify their visual experiences. Have children predict what they will see when surfaces are magnified and record their predictions. Then have them describe through pictures and stories what they actually saw.

◇ **Reflecting**

Children can organize their experiences by using large areas of the classroom to display their experiments with the senses, their journals, charts reflecting sensory perceptions, and artwork. The activities previously suggested require the creation of various learning centers that children may revisit to reflect upon their work. Teachers will want to discuss with small groups of children the results of their sensory investigations and explorations.

Have a party for family members to experiment with the senses. Use the centers and activities described here, and have the children suggest directions to post for families so that they may also use their senses in an environment that provides several and varied interactive experiences. Since food is highly sensory, have lots of different food available for families to taste and enjoy. Both children and the cooking staff can prepare the meal. Help children to make the food visually appealing by adding decorative touches. Children may ask family members if they can identify the ingredients that were part of each recipe. Give everyone a chance to admire the interesting centers and the charts of new vocabulary words. (See tear-out sheet 1 on p. 129.)

◇ **Extending and Expanding to the Early Primary Grades**

Children in the early primary grades can do the following:

◆ Understand that the senses work together. For example, the nose is responsible for part of the flavor of food. So, ask children to hold their noses closed, and use just their tongues to identify what they are eating. Give them something like a pear or apple slice. They may have trouble telling you what it is. Also ask them to distinguish one food from another. Have them try again with their nose open. They will probably get it right. Baby food is an excellent vehicle for testing how the senses work together.

◆ Associate their senses with the parts of the body that they represent. Discuss how each of the senses functions. Show children a model of the ear, for example, and explain how it conducts sound.

◆ Build a larger and more complex scientific vocabulary pertaining to the senses.

◆ Appreciate their senses and learn how to care for them properly. Have children generate ideas on how to protect their hearing (ears) and vision (eyes), or name safety hazards to the eyes and ears. Chart these and have the children turn them into safety rules for the classroom.

◆   Access Web sites for information on the senses.

◆   Read *A Picture Book of Louis Braille* by David Adler. Discuss Braille's remarkable achievements and let the children close their eyes and try reading using the braille alphabet. This will take practice. Have them write a short story using perforations instead of the usual implements.

◆   Read *A Picture Book of Helen Keller* by David Adler. Have the children predict what Helen will be able to do without two of her senses. Then have them imagine how they could learn using their other senses. Have them prepare short dramatizations of Helen Keller's life.

◇ Documenting Children's Learning

A web can document the concepts, learnings, skills, and attitudes that children have developed through their active sensory experiences. Teachers will want children and parents to take part in generating various sections of the web. This will assist with reflection and recall and help to cement the home-school connection. Parents may also want to create their own webs based on the home activities that they do with their children.

Children's experiences are further documented through their vocabulary and comparison charts and their labeled displays. These should remain in the classroom for children to reflect upon and generate new concepts.

Science Exhibit and Party
Everyone Come!
Baby-Sitting, Cooking, and Refreshments

Date

Dear Parents:

We are about to conclude our thematic unit on the senses. During this time, we focused on activities and experiences designed to help your children understand how we learn through the senses. In fact, we are dependent on one or more of our senses for all of the information that we acquire. We have conducted many experiments, indoors and outdoors, to use the senses in understanding the world around us. We hope that you have enjoyed your listening and observing walks with your children and any cooking you may have done together. Just alerting your children to observe things more closely and describe them using their senses helps us with our work.

Now it is time to have a party to celebrate the many things we have accomplished during this unit. It was fun and hard work too. Your whole family is invited, and transportation will be provided for anyone who needs it. Just drop us a note.

On _____ at _____ in the _____ at school, we will be having a science party. The event will include exhibits and experiments that your children have prepared for you to highlight the senses. They have made directions for you to follow as you explore many things using all of your senses. There will also be several simple cooking stations where you will be invited to join your children in describing ingredients before, during, and after they are cooked together. Books about the senses will be displayed for you to examine, and we will have music with distinct sounds. If you have a favorite tape or CD, please bring it along.

There will be plenty of refreshments to enjoy. We thank you again for working with us and look forward to seeing you at the party.

Sincerely,

Group Observation—Science Vocabulary
(These terms refer to the five senses.)

Date:

Center/Outside:

Children's Names:

Science Terms Used (Record terms on the left)

Accuracy

	Not at All	Some	Accurate
1.	_____	_____	_____
2.	_____	_____	_____
3.	_____	_____	_____
4.	_____	_____	_____
5.	_____	_____	_____
6.	_____	_____	_____
7.	_____	_____	_____
8.	_____	_____	_____
9.	_____	_____	_____
10.	_____	_____	_____

Comments:

Date _____

Name _____

Age of Child _____

Individual Evaluation: Assessing Children's Science Skills
The Human Body: The Senses

	Always	Sometimes	Never
Can name the five senses	_____	_____	_____
Associates each sense with the correct parts of the human body	_____	_____	_____
Uses one or more of the five senses to discover properties of things in the environment	_____	_____	_____
Compares things using only one sense	_____	_____	_____
Classifies things using only one sense	_____	_____	_____
Describes how two or more senses work together	_____	_____	_____
Appreciates the senses as a learning tool (can describe how something is being learned)	_____	_____	_____
Demonstrates an understanding of what it is like to have a sensory impairment	_____	_____	_____
Demonstrates an understanding of persons with sensory impairments	_____	_____	_____
Asks appropriate questions	_____	_____	_____
Participates in sensory experiments	_____	_____	_____
Makes appropriate predictions and conclusions	_____	_____	_____
Uses reference books	_____	_____	_____
Writes stories about the senses	_____	_____	_____
Uses senses to describe indoor/ outdoor environment	_____	_____	_____

Additional Comments:

8

Healthy Bodies

FOR THE TEACHER

◇ **What You'll Need to Know**

Young children should have a variety of experiences that provide initial understanding of personal health. They are anxious to grow and become strong, but teachers should be aware of the concepts and misconceptions they have about health. Most children attribute all illnesses to germs without an understanding of the different origins of disease, and the prevention and cure of disease. Children *do* link eating with growth, health, strength, and energy, but they do not necessarily understand that (and why) some foods are nutritionally better than others. Additionally, they are eager to learn about their bodies inside and out, but they have worries about body images and differences between their development and that of others.

With the help and guidance of teachers and parents, young children need to become individuals who have a lifelong responsibility for their own health and personal care including dental hygiene, cleanliness, and exercise. Some early childhood educators have noticed that despite recommendations for good nutrition, changing family lifestyles are having an adverse impact on the nutritional habits of many young children. More sugar and fat now enter their diets, and many cooking activities suggested for classroom use do not include nutritional learning objectives. Thus, parents and teachers should be committed to the premise that the care and nourishment of the human body is essential to the well-being of children and the content of a science program. Be sure to inform parents about your emphasis on healthy bodies and enlist their help in maintaining good health practices in the home.

◇ **Key Concepts**

- Each person is unique with a special body type.

- Lungs help us to breathe and use the oxygen in the air.

- Bones support our bodies and help them keep their shape.

- Our hearts are a special part of our body.

- We depend on muscles to move every part of the human body.

- The food pyramid offers many choices of good foods to keep our bodies healthy.

- We must eat foods from each of the major food groups in order to stay healthy.

- We help ourselves stay healthy and grow strong by contributing to our own personal care.

◇ **Goals and Objectives**

Children will appreciate their uniqueness by describing their bodies and comparing themselves with others.

Children will examine simple diagrams of the lungs and learn how they operate through exercises using the lungs.

Children will recognize that bone structure supports the body by examining a model or an illustration of the skeleton.

Children will identify the heart as a muscle.

Children will learn that bone structure and body actions are related.

Children will identify the feeling of muscles in many parts of the body.

Children will recognize and appreciate nourishing foods.

Children will plan a healthy, balanced diet.

Children will recognize the health contribution of different foods.

Children will grow and eat nutritious foods.

Children will be willing to try new foods.

Children will assume responsibility for washing their hands and brushing their teeth.

◇ What You'll Need

Books For Adults and Older Children

The following books are primarily for much older children and provide an excellent background for the early childhood teacher on the body and how it functions.

Baird, P. (1994). *The pyramid cookbook.* New York: Henry Holt.

Cole, J. (1992). *Your insides.* New York: Putnam.

Ganeri, A. (1994). *Eating.* Austin, TX: Raintree.

Ganeri, A. (1994). *Moving.* Austin, TX: Raintree.

Morrison, L. (1997). *I scream, you scream: A feast of food rhymes.* Little Rock, AR: August House.

Parker, S. (1998). *The human body: And how it works.* New York: Dorling Kindersley.

Parsons, A. (1996). *Fit for life.* Danbury, CN: Watts.

Patent, D. (1993). *Nutrition.* New York: Holiday House.

Powell, J. (1998). *Exercise and your health.* Austin, TX: Raintree.

Sandeman, A. (1995). *Breathing.* Brookfield, CT: Copper Beech.

Children's Books

Adler, D. (1991). *You breathe in, you breathe out: All about your lungs.* Danbury, CN: Watts.

Berger, M. (1983). *Why I cough, sneeze, shiver, hiccup, & yawn.* New York: Harper Collins.

Berger, M. (1989). *Germs make me sick.* New York: Harper.

Cole, J. (1998). *The magic schoolbus: Inside the human body.* New York: Putnam.

Curtis, J. L. (1993). *When I was little; A four year old's memoir of her youth.* New York: HarperCollins.

Dooley, N. (1991). *Everyone cooks rice.* Minneapolis: Carolrhoda Books.

Hausherr, R. (1994). *What food is this?* New York: Scholastic.

Hoban, R. (1986). *Bread and jam for Frances.* New York: Harper Collins.

Hoban, T. (1976). *Big ones, little ones.* New York: Greenwillow Books.

Hoberman, M. A. (1997). *The seven silly eaters.* San Diego: Harcourt Brace.

Leedy, L. (1994). *The edible pyramid: Good eating every day.* New York: Holiday House.

Morris, A. (1989). *Bread, bread, bread.* New York: Scholastic.

Sandeman, A. (1995). *Bones.* Copper Beach.

Sharmat, M. (1980). *Gregory the terrible eater.* New York: Macmillan.

Showers, P. (1982). *You can't make a move without your muscles.* New York: Harper.

Other Things You'll Need

- Illustrations of the human body and/or a plastic model of the skeleton
- Chicken bones
- Stethoscopes
- Chart paper
- Markers and crayons
- Large mirror
- Yardstick or tape measure
- Scale
- Stiff cards and paper
- Scissors
- Glue
- Dirty fabrics
- Soap
- Dishpans
- Water
- Potting soil and containers for planting an inside or outside garden
- Simple food guide pyramid (Figure 13–1)
- Cooking utensils and cooking source
- Magazines for collage
- Props to turn creative dramatic area into a restaurant

◇ **The Home-School Connection**

Today's busy families often sacrifice sleep, exercise, and a healthy balanced diet because of the multiple commitments to work and the many facets of family life. Families are partners in this area of the science curriculum since they set the stage for their children's healthy development. Every day is filled with opportunities to foster healthy development. A child's bad cold can be turned into a chance to learn science. Parents can

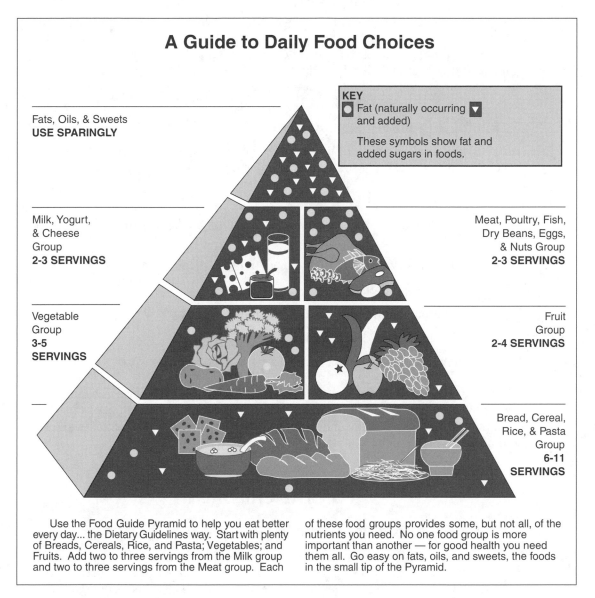

A Guide to Daily Food Choices

KEY
⬤ Fat (naturally occurring ▼
and added)

These symbols show fat and
added sugars in foods.

Fats, Oils, & Sweets
USE SPARINGLY

Milk, Yogurt,
& Cheese
Group
2-3 SERVINGS

Meat, Poultry, Fish,
Dry Beans, Eggs,
& Nuts Group
2-3 SERVINGS

Vegetable
Group
**3-5
SERVINGS**

Fruit
Group
2-4 SERVINGS

Bread, Cereal,
Rice, & Pasta
Group
**6-11
SERVINGS**

Use the Food Guide Pyramid to help you eat better every day... the Dietary Guidelines way. Start with plenty of Breads, Cereals, Rice, and Pasta; Vegetables; and Fruits. Add two to three servings from the Milk group and two to three servings from the Meat group. Each of these food groups provides some, but not all, of the nutrients you need. No one food group is more important than another — for good health you need them all. Go easy on fats, oils, and sweets, the foods in the small tip of the Pyramid.

FIGURE 13–1
Food guide pyramid

read simple books on how diseases are passed from person to person. This sets the stage for the enforcing of simple rules such as regular tooth brushing and hand washing. These routines become hassle free when children practice them early at home.

Or—parents can teach some ways to stay healthy such as not sharing forks, spoons, or glasses, and covering our nose and mouth when we sneeze or cough. There are many fine cookbooks with simple healthy recipes that parents and children can try together. The book *Everyone Cooks Rice* by N. Dooley not only may provide a shared experience, but conveys positive images of other cultures to children. A pictorial food pyramid can hang on the refrigerator as a reminder of foods that children should sample often and others that we save for special occasions because, although they may be pleasant to eat, they don't help us grow well, strong, and healthy.

A regular trip to the food store will allow children to pick from the various food groups. For older children, bags may be labeled ahead so that children can select the foods themselves and place them into the containers. Within a food group, there are always favorites.

Finally, families can encourage children to feel good about their bodies and body image. Children's growth may be charted on an unobtrusive wall or chart paper. Parents should encourage their children to view themselves and discuss their positive attributes.

◇   **Evaluating and Assessing Children's Learning**

Assessing children's concepts of the body, how it works, and how to keep it healthy will be a continuous process done on an individual and group basis using

- teacher observations

- individual and group discussions with children as they work individually or in groups

- structured interviews with children about the particular concept under study

- portfolios of children's work

- examination of children's pictures, diagrams, and stories

- examination of any data recorded

- children's self-evaluations of their interest level and their work

The tear-out sheets on pages 142–143 at the end of this chapter can be used at different times in the school year to chart growth in children's knowledge of their bodies and how to keep them healthy and to help you plan your curriculum to extend and expand upon children's current understandings.

——————————   **FOR THE CHILDREN**   ——————————

◇   **Indoor and Outdoor Activities**

The teacher will want to emphasize the theme of healthy bodies throughout the various centers of the classroom by using displays of children's fiction and informational books, posters, photographs, diagrams, and plastic models of the body, if possible. To stimulate children's interest and concept formation, active experiences may be constructed for centers such as a restaurant in the dramatic play area that serves a balanced and nutritious diet.

◆   Have each child make a book entitled *All About Me*. The format may vary from child to child. The children may include a self-portrait after looking in the mirror, their height, their weight, the things they like to eat, how long they like to sleep, and other items related to health. They may want to add pages as the year progresses to chart their growth. Each child may dictate a story explaining what makes him different from other class members and how they are the same.

◆   Read *You Breathe In, You Breathe Out: All About Your Lungs* by D. Adler. Point out the simple diagram explaining how we breathe. Have the children place their hands on their chest and take a deep breath. Ask if they can feel their chest get bigger as their lungs fill with air. Then have them exhale, or let the air out. Do their chest and lungs get smaller? Have small groups of children exercise outside. Does their breathing get faster? The teacher may chart the answers to these and other questions.

◆ To emphasize the need to keep the air that we breathe clean, have children take index cards and tape them to various places inside and outside the classroom. On each card they can put a small amount of petroleum jelly. After a few days, have the children note the amount of pollutants that have built up on each card. Ask them which cards have the most and why they think so.

◆ Read selected parts of *Bones* by A. Sandeman. Remind the children that without bones to hold their organs in place, their body would collapse. Do a movement activity that involves collapsing and getting up again using various bones and muscles. Have children get in pairs. When one child curls up tight, have the other feel small bones in the spine and vice versa. Have children dictate and illustrate a story about the bones they can feel and how they feel and bend differently.

◆ Acquire a plastic skeleton or make a visit to a clinic or doctor's office where children can observe and describe one.

◆ Take a trip to a natural history museum where the bones of various animals are exhibited. Have children prepare a list of things that they want to know. After returning to the classroom, list on chart paper the facts that children now know.

◆ Save chicken bones from mealtime (and have children bring them in). Put them on the science table and have children examine and describe them. How do the bones differ from their own and the others that they have observed?

◆ Read selections of *You Can't Make a Move Without Your Muscles* by P. Showers. Have children go to the carpeted section of the classroom or use exercise mats. Ask them what they know about muscles and record their answers. Then ask them to do a series of movements to feel the muscles working in their bodies. Movements may include moving their fingers off the floor, stretching their arms to reach the "sky," trying to touch their toes with their legs in a straight position, and curling up tightly and then unwinding. Finally, have them make different faces. Do they need muscles to smile? To frown?

◆ Acquire a stethoscope or visit a clinic or doctor's office. Have children pair up and listen to each other's heart. Children can listen through paper tubes if no stethoscope is available. If the children are able, count heartbeats for about thirty seconds when the children are at rest and then after exercise. Have the children dictate a story about their observations.

◆ Read *The Edible Pyramid: Good Eating Every Day* by L. Leedy. The Edible Pyramid is a restaurant that serves a variety of nutritious meals. The animals at the restaurant are introduced to the food groups shown in the nutritional pyramid. Have children design a collage using old magazines. Hang a nutritional pyramid in the classroom. (It can be pictorial with labels.) Ask children to make sure that each food group is represented.

◆   Plan a visit to a good local restaurant. Speak with the owner in advance and ask her to explain how she chooses from nutritious foods to make delicious meals. Have children choose a nutritious meal keeping the ingredients of each dish in mind.

◆   Providing tables and eating utensils, create a restaurant in the creative dramatic corner. Have children decide on a name and design menus, placemats, napkins, and decorations. Provide pads and pencils to take orders and make out checks. Extend this project as far as the children want to go. Create signs, plan shopping trips to the local market, cook and serve real food, and invite guests to sample the children's healthy and well-balanced meals. Foods can vary across cultures as children are exposed to various cookbooks. Be sure to respect the dietary laws and customs of different cultures. Concepts of money may be integrated by using prices on the menus and exchanging money for goods.

◆   Create a theme store such as a bakery. Read *Bread, Bread, Bread* by A. Morris and bake breads from different countries. Have children design a take-out menu to be distributed to small groups of parents or children at a time. Sell the bread and use the proceeds for nutritious foods.

◆   Plant a garden inside or outside. This, too, will be an extended project. Children may cook the vegetables and grains, watch how they are transformed in the cooking process, and serve them in the restaurant or as a treat for parents and the school director.

◆   Children are very interested in germs. Find out what they know. What they may not know is that the germs that cause illness are too small to see. Have the children experiment to find out how to get those germs off their hands by washing with soap and water. In the science center, provide dirty fabric, two dishpans, soap, and water. Have children wash one piece of fabric just with water and the other with soap and water (this can be repeated as children come to the center). Let the fabric dry and compare the two samples. Children may record findings in their science journals.

◇   Reflecting

Ask children to organize their experiences by providing them with an area of the classroom where they can display their journals, "About Me" books, charts, and explanations of experiments. Add menus, homegrown and cooked food, and props children have created for their restaurant or bakery.

Have a party for family members to sample the foods the children have grown in the garden as well as breads and nutritionally balanced meals created for the restaurant. Parents and siblings will enjoy the fruits of their labor.

◇   Extending and Expanding to the Early Primary Grades

Children in the early primary grades can do the following:

◆   Draw a story line about a day in their lives from the time they woke up until they went to sleep at night. Include all the health and safety things they did. The teacher may write questions on poster board: When did you wash your hands? Did you brush your teeth after each meal? In the morning? At night? Did you take a shower or a bath? What situations occurred that caused you to think about safety? They can discuss the importance of health precautions and safety.

◆ Classify foods into food groups. Place foods, food replicas, or empty food cartons into bags labeled with the six food groups, or on a large poster or table depicting the food pyramid. They can match the food to the description of the food group. For example, Breads and Grains = These provide energy and fiber. We need to eat the most from this group. This would be a good game to play with family members at a party.

◆ Make copies of one week's menus from the school cafeteria. Discuss if they meet the criteria set by the food pyramid.

◆ Learn about their teeth by making a map by carefully biting into an apple slice. Describe the different marks and learn the terms for different teeth. Finally, discuss the reasons for needing different kinds of teeth.

◆ Understand the reasons why the classroom should be clean and safe. In small groups or as a total group experience, children can make rules that will ensure cleanliness and safety. The rules should be recorded, hung in the classroom, and modified when necessary.

◆ Acquire more sophisticated knowledge of the body. Read *The Magic Schoolbus: Inside the Human Body* by J. Cole. Have children draw parts of the body and label them.

◆ Understand why it is necessary to drink water. They can record the amount of water they drink each day and determine whether it conforms to the prescribed standards for their body.

◆ Utilize computers to locate the Web sites of science museums, the Department of Agriculture, and other resources for children. Teachers will want to make sure that the sites are suitable.

◆ Build a larger working vocabulary of scientific terms related to healthy bodies. These may be recorded in their science journals and posted by experiments for easy reference.

◆ Create a bulletin board on the thematic unit of healthy bodies.

◆ Learn to be sensitive to environmental issues and take action to support a healthy environment. Read *The Great Kapok Tree* by L. Cherry and *Recycle! A Handbook for Kids* by G. Gibbons. The first book should help children to understand the interconnectedness of elements of the environment. The second should inspire children to recycle at home, in the classroom, and in the community. Children can be encouraged to write letters to their principal, to the mayor of their town or city, or even to Congress or the president about environmental issues that concern them.

◇ Documenting Children's Learning

A web can document the concepts, learnings, skills, and attitudes that children develop during their study of healthy bodies. Several webs might be generated on topics such as body parts, foods we eat, staying healthy, and environmental concerns.

"About Me" books created by the children and a bulletin board with drawings and pictures of the restaurant and bakery will help children to recall their new concepts about healthy bodies. Children may be encouraged to create a newsletter for parents and members of the school community to explain how to stay healthy and to suggest ways to improve on the school and community environments.

Date _____

Name _____

Age of Child _____

Individual Evaluation: Assessing Children's Science Skills
Healthy Bodies

	Always	Sometimes	Never
Describes own body	_____	_____	_____
Compares own body to those of other children	_____	_____	_____
Appears to be satisfied with body image	_____	_____	_____
Examines simple diagrams of the lungs	_____	_____	_____
Participates in exercises using the lungs	_____	_____	_____
Examines models or illustrations of the skeleton	_____	_____	_____
Recognizes that bone structure supports the body	_____	_____	_____
Identifies the heart as a muscle	_____	_____	_____
Discovers that bone structure and body actions are related	_____	_____	_____
Discusses the feeling of muscles in parts of the body	_____	_____	_____
Identifies nourishing foods	_____	_____	_____
Discusses the value of nourishing foods	_____	_____	_____
Plans a healthy, balanced diet	_____	_____	_____
Grows nutritious foods	_____	_____	_____
Is willing to try new, nutritious foods	_____	_____	_____
Assumes responsibility for washing hands	_____	_____	_____
Assumes responsibility for brushing teeth	_____	_____	_____
Reads books about healthy bodies	_____	_____	_____
Consults reference books about healthy bodies	_____	_____	_____
Writes stories about healthy bodies	_____	_____	_____
Asks appropriate questions	_____	_____	_____

Additional Comments:

Permission is granted by the publisher to reproduce this page.

Group Observation—Science Terms
(These terms refer to healthy bodies.)

Date:

Center/Outside:

Children's Names:

Science Terms Used (Record terms on the left)

	Accuracy		
	Not at All	Some	Accurate
1.	_____	_____	_____
2.	_____	_____	_____
3.	_____	_____	_____
4.	_____	_____	_____
5.	_____	_____	_____
6.	_____	_____	_____
7.	_____	_____	_____
8.	_____	_____	_____
9.	_____	_____	_____
10.	_____	_____	_____

Comments:

References

American Association for the Advancement of Science. (1989). *Science for all Americans.* New York: Oxford University Press.

American Association for the Advancement of Science. (1993). *Benchmarks for science literacy.* New York: Oxford University Press.

American Association for the Advancement of Science. (1998). *Forum on early childhood science, mathematics, and technology education.* Washington, DC: Author.

Barclay, K., Benelli, C., & Schoon, S. (1999). Making the connection! Science and literature. *Childhood Education, 75,* 146–152.

Barclay, K., & Traser, L. (1999). Supporting young researchers as they write to learn. *Childhood Education, 75,* 215–224.

Berk, L. E., & Winsler, A. (1995). *Scaffolding children's learning: Vygotsky and early childhood education.* Washington, DC: National Association for the Education of Young Children.

Blaska, J. K., & Lynch, E. C. (1998). Is everyone included? Using children's literature to facilitate the understanding of disabilities. *Young Children, 53*(2), 36–40.

Bredekamp, S. (1993, November). Reflections on Reggio Emilia. *Young Children,* p. 13.

Bredekamp, S., & Copple, C. (Eds.). (1997). *Developmentally appropriate practice in early childhood programs* (rev. ed.). Washington, DC: National Association for the Education of Young Children.

Bredekamp, S., & Rosegrant, T. (1995). *Reaching potentials: Transforming early childhood curriculum and assessment* (Vol. 2). Washington, DC: National Association for the Education of Young Children.

Brewer, J. A. (1998). *Introduction to early childhood education: Preschool through primary grades* (3rd ed.). Boston: Allyn & Bacon.

Bronfenbrenner, U. (1979). *The ecology of human development: Experiments by nature and design.* Cambridge, MA: Harvard University Press.

Bronson, M. B. (1995). *The right stuff.* Washington, DC: National Association for the Education of Young Children.

Davis, J. (2001). The day Pork Chop died (almost). Caregivers Corner. *Young Children, 56*(3), 85.

Dewey, J. (1938). *Experience and education.* New York: Collier Books.

Dewey, J. (1944). *Democracy and education.* New York: The Free Press.

Dighe, J., Calomiris, Z., & Van Zutphen, C. (1998). Nurturing the language of art in children. *Young Children, 53*(1), 4–9.

Donoghue, M. R. (2001). *Using literature activities to teach content areas to emergent readers.* Needham Heights, MA: Allyn & Bacon.

Galvin, E. S. (1994). The joy of seasons: With the children, discover the joys of nature. *Young Children, 49*(4), 4–9.

Grolnick, W. S., & Slowiaczek, M. L. (1994). Parents' involvement in children's schooling: A multi-dimensional conceptualization and motivational model. *Child Development, 65,* 237–252.

Harlan, J. D., & Rivkin, M. S. (2000). *Science experiences for the early childhood years: An integrated approach* (7th ed.). Upper Saddle River, NJ: Merrill/Prentice Hall.

Helm, J. H., & Katz, L. G. (2001). *Young investigators: The project approach in the early years.* New York: Teachers College Press/Washington, DC: National Association for the Education of Young Children.

Henniger, M. L. (1994). Planning for outdoor play. *Young Children, 49*(4), 10–15.

Katz, L. (1993). What can we learn from Reggio Emilia? In C. Edwards, L. Gandini, & G. Forman (Eds.), *The hundred languages of children* (pp. 19–41). Norwood, NJ: Ablex.

Kilmer, S. J., & Hofman, H. (1995). In S. Bredekamp & T. Rosegrant (Eds.), *Reaching potentials: Transforming early childhood curriculum and assessment* (Vol. 2, pp. 43–63). Washington, DC: National Association for the Education of Young Children.

Loughlin, C., & Suina, J. (1982). *The learning environment: An instructional strategy.* New York: Teachers College Press.

Lowery, L. (Ed.). (1997). *NSTA pathways to the science standard: Elementary school edition.* Arlington, VA.: National Science Teachers Association.

Mallory, B. L. (1998). Educating young children with developmental differences: Principles of inclusive practice. In C. Seefeldt & A. Galper (Eds.), *Continuing issues in early childhood education* (2nd ed., p. 228). Upper Saddle River, NJ: Merrill/Prentice Hall.

Mallory, B. L., & New, R. S. (1994). *Diversity & developmentally appropriate practices: Challenges to early childhood education.* New York: Teachers College Press.

Marcon, R. (1992). Differential effects of three preschool models on inner-city 4-year-olds. *Early Childhood Research Quarterly, 7,* 517–530.

National Academy of Sciences. (1995). *National science education standards.* Washington, DC: Author.

National Research Council. (1996). *National science education standards.* Washington, DC: National Academy Press.

Paulu, N. (1992). *Helping your child learn science.* Washington, DC: U.S. Department of Education: Office of Educational Research and Improvement.

Piaget, J. (1954). *The construction of reality in the child.* New York: Basic Books.

Piaget, J. (1973). *The children's conception of the world.* St. Albans: Paladin.

Powell, D. R. (1989). Families and early childhood programs. *Research Monographs of the National Association for the Education of Young Children, 3.*

Rivkin, M. S. (1995). *The great outdoors: Restoring children's right to play outside.* Washington, DC: National Association for the Education of Young Children.

Seefeldt, C. (1995). Art: A serious work. *Young Children, 50*(3), 39–54.

Seefeldt, C. (1997). *Social studies for the preschool-primary child.* Upper Saddle River, NJ: Merrill/Prentice Hall.

Seefeldt, C., & Barbour, N. (1998). *Early childhood education: An introduction.* Upper Saddle River, NJ: Merrill/Prentice Hall.

Seefeldt, C., & Galper, A. (2000). *Active experiences for active children: Social studies.* Upper Saddle River, NJ: Merrill/Prentice Hall.

Stevenson, D. L., & Baker, D. P. (1987), The family-school relations and the child's school performance. *Child Development, 58,* 1348–1357.

Swick, K. J. (1997). Learning about work: Extending learning through an ecological approach. In B. Hatcher & S. S. Beck (Eds.), *Learning opportunities beyond the school* (2nd ed., pp. 37–43). Olney MD: Association for Childhood Education International.

Vygotsky, L. (1978). *Thought and language.* Cambridge, MA: MIT Press.

Vygotsky, L. (1986). *Thought and language* (rev. ed.). Cambridge, MA: MIT Press.

Wenner, G. (1993). Relationship between science knowledge levels and beliefs toward science instruction held by preservice elementary teachers. *Journal of Science Education and Technology, 2,* 461–468.

Wilson, R. A. (1995). Nature and young children: A natural connection. *Young Children, 50*(6), 4–7.

Wright, J. L., & Shade, D. D. (1994). *Young children: Active learners in a technological age.* Washington, DC: National Association for the Education of Young Children.

Youniss, J., & Damon, W. (1992). Social construction of Piaget's theory. In H. Beilin & P. B. Pufall (Eds.), *Piaget's theory: Prospects and possibilities.* Hillsdale, NJ: Erlbaum.

Resources

Organizations and Web Sites

American Association for the Advancement of Science
1200 New York Avenue NW
Washington, DC 20005
202-326-6400
http://www.aaas.org/contact.html
Project 2061, Benchmarks for Science Literacy can be reached by telephone at 202-326-6666.
The American Association for the Advancement of Science reviews science books for children in *Science Books and Films.* For a subscription, write to SB&F Subscriptions, AAAS, Room 814, 1333 H Street, NW, Washington, DC 20005.

The Children's School of Science
P.O. Box 552
Woods Hole, MA 02543
http://www.capecod.com/whcss/about.html
The Children's School of Science attempts to build a love and an appreciation of science by exercising the child's natural curiosity. Their mission involves direct observation and understanding. The projects in the following excellent book are adapted from their program:
The Children's School of Science (1997). *The big book of nature projects.* New York: Thames and Hudson.

Consumer Information Center
Pueblo, CO 81009
There are many booklets and pamphlets available for free or for a small fee. The catalogue is free. The CIC also publishes "Books for Children," an annual listing from the Library of Congress of the best books recently published for preschool through junior high school-age children. It includes books on science and nature.

Corporation for Public Broadcasting (PBS)
http://www.pbs.org/teachersource/science

ERIC Clearinghouse
Children's Literature in the Science Classroom
http://www.indiana.edu
Many good ideas for children's books of all types to integrate with science lessons.

Lawrence Hall of Sciences
Berkeley, CA 94720-5200
510-642-5132
FAX 510-642-1055
Lawrence Hall of Science is the public science center and the center for school change, teacher education, and curriculum development at the University of California at Berkeley. Teaching materials and outreach science programs for preschool through high school emphasize the interactive, inquiry-based approach to learning.
www.lhs.berkeley.edu

National Geographic Society
17th and M Streets, NW
Washington, DC 20036
Publishes *National Geographic World.*
There is also an excellent science Web site for children (and teachers):
http://www.nationalgeographic.com/kids/

National Science Teachers Association
1840 Wilson Boulevard
Arlington, VA 22201
703-243-7177
FAX 703-243-7177
Responsible for the Science Standards, the National Science Teachers Association also publishes educational products and activity books for students from kindergarten through college.
www.nsta.org

The Children's Book Council and the National Science Teachers Association cite outstanding science trade books for children. A list is available by sending a request and a stamped, self-addressed envelope to
National Science Teacher's Association
Public Information Office
1742 Connecticut Avenue NW
Washington, DC 20009.

US Department of Agriculture, Food and Nutrition Services, Team Nutrition
http://www.fns.usda.gov/tn/Resources/goglowgrow.html
Team nutrition provides educational materials for teachers and children. Two excellent resources for preschool aged children are *Go Glow Grow: Foods for You,* a colorful, interactive nutrition activity booklet for 3 and 4-year olds, and a food pyramid to hang in the classroom. Call 1-800-321-3054.

U.S. Fish and Wildlife Service
http://www.fws.gov
This site offers written materials and suggestions for conservation and conservation education. The teacher can also click on "Most Frequently Asked Questions."

U.S. Government: Helping Your Child Learn Science
http://www.ed.gov/pubs/parents/Science/Resources.html
Excellent list of resources for parents (and teachers).

Magazines

3-2-1-Contact, Children's Television Workshop, One Lincoln Plaza, New York, NY 10023.

Ladybug, Cricket Country Lane, Box 50284, Boulder, CO 80321-0284.

Ranger Rick, National Wildlife Federation, 1412 16th Street, NW, Washington, DC 20036-2266.

Equipment Sources

Delta Education, Inc.
P.O. Box 3000
Nashua, NH 03061-3000
Hands-on equipment and materials for children kindergarten through 8 on the areas of Earth Sciences, Life Sciences, and Physical Sciences.

Lawrence Hall of Science (see earlier reference)

Index

Ackerman, D., 120
Adler, D., 135, 138
Adler, David, 128
Agler, L., 97
Alexander and the Wind-up Mouse (Lionni), 89, 90
Aliki, 109, 121, 122
American Association for the Advancement of
    Science, 4, 5, 7, 11, 22, 23, 25, 40, 41, 42,
    43, 109
Animals in the Classroom (Kramer), 67
Animals. *See* Insects and small animals;
    Insects/small animals experiences
Animals That Hibernate (Brimmer), 73
Ant Cities (Dorros), 67
Anthropomorphism, 67, 71
Ardley, N., 120
Art activities, 24, 55
Art centers, 14–15
Asch, F., 67
Assessment
    children as scientists experiences and, 82
    healthy bodies experiences and, 138, 142
    how toys work experiences and, 89
    insects/small animals experiences and, 69, 77
    of prior knowledge, 4, 43
    rocks/minerals experiences and, 111, 117
    seeds/plants experiences and, 52, 62
    senses experiences and, 122–123, 131
    types of, 6
    water experiences and, 99, 103
Association for Childhood Education
    International, 43
Autumn Leaves (Robbins), 51

Baby Bird's First Nest (Asch), 67
Backyard Birdwatcher, The (Harrison), 67
Baird, P., 135
Baker, D. P., 36
Baldwin, A. N., 51, 55
Ballard, C., 121
Barbour, N., 11, 12
Barclay, K., 41, 44
Baylor, B., 13, 109
Bear Loves Water (Weiss), 97
Benchmarks for Science Literacy (American
    Association for the Advancement of
    Science), 4, 5, 7, 11, 23, 25, 40, 42, 43

Benelli, C., 44
Berenstain, S., 51, 54
Berenstain Bears Grow It, The (Berenstain), 51, 54
Berger, G., 97, 101
Berger, M., 97, 101, 135
Berk, L. E., 19, 30
Best Book of Fossils, Rocks, and Minerals
    (Pellant), 109
Big Ones, Little Ones (Hoban), 136
Blaska, J. K., 15
Block areas, 17
Bones (Sandeman), 136, 139
Book and library centers, 15–16
Booth, B., 121, 124
Brandt, K., 97
Branley, F. M., 97, 101
Bread, Bread, Bread (Morris), 136, 140
Bread and Jam for Frances (Hoban), 135
Breathing (Sandeman), 135
Bredekamp, S., 12, 36, 38, 40, 45
Brewer, J. A., 37, 38
Brimmer, L. D., 73
Bronfenbrenner, U., 30
Bronson, M. B., 13
Brown Bear, Brown Bear, What Do You See?
    (Martin and Carle), 121
Bugs (Parker and Wright), 67
Bumie, D., 121
Buried Treasure (Hughes and Hughes), 51
Busbey, A. B., 110
Butterfly Alphabet, The (Sandved), 68
Butzow, C. M., 97
Butzow, J. W., 97
By the Seashore (Pledger), 97

Cain, J., 97
Callister, J. C., 97, 109
Calomiris, Z., 14
Carle, E., 51, 54, 67, 121
Carlstrom, N., 51, 54
Centers of interest, 12
Cherry, L., 141
Children's Book Council, 51
Children's books. *See* Children's literature;
    Literary resources
Children as scientists experiences, 80–85
    assessment and, 82

Children as scientists experiences—*Cont.*
  documenting children's learning, 85
  goals and objectives, 80
  home involvement and, 81–82
  investigations and, 80, 84–85
  key concepts, 80
  literary resources, 81
  observation and, 80, 82–83
  questioning and, 80, 83–84
  science subject matter and, 41
  supplies for, 80–81
  teaching strategies for, 80–82
Children's growth and development
  assessment of, 43
  cognitive development, 5–6, 12, 40
  firsthand experiences and, 44
  home involvement and, 136–137
  inclusion and, 12
  life sciences and, 50
  universal patterns of, 40
Children's interests and needs, 31
Children's literature
  book and library centers and, 15–16
  field activities and, 33
  firsthand experiences and, 44
  healthy bodies experiences and, 135–136
  how toys work experiences and, 89
  insects/small animals experiences and,
    67–68, 71
  integrated curriculum and, 13, 15
  rocks/minerals experiences and, 109–110
  seeds/plants experiences and, 51, 54–55
  senses experiences and, 121
  water experiences and, 97–98
Children with special needs. *See also* Inclusion
  book and library centers and, 15
  inclusion and, 11–12
  senses experiences and, 120, 123
Christian, P., 109, 110
Classroom pets, 71–72
Coenraads, R. R., 110
Cognitive development, 5–6, 12, 40
Cole, J., 135, 141
Collaborative participation, 7, 27, 44
Collard, Sneed B., 51
Community resources, 30, 32–33, 35–36
Computers
  computer stations, 18
  enhancing firsthand experiences with, 45
  insects/small animals experiences and, 72
  seeds/plants experiences and, 56
  water experiences and, 102
Conceptual learning
  art activities and, 24
  building concepts, 6
  children's literature and, 15–16
  community resources and, 30
  hands-on learning and, 40

indoor learning environment and, 12, 19
  insects/small animals experiences and, 68
Concise Encyclopedia of the Human Body, The
    (Bumie), 121
Constructivism, 5, 41, 50
Content integrity and meaning, 5
Content standards, 4–5. *See also specific standards*
Continuity of experience, 31
Cooperation, 22–23
Copple, C., 36, 40
Creepy Crawlies and the Scientific Method
    (Kneidel), 67
Cromwell, S., 121
Crowder, J. N., 97
Cultural diversity
  book and library centers and, 15
  field activities and, 32
  home involvement and, 36, 37
  science subject matter and, 41
Culture acquiring, 30
Curious George Flies a Kite (Rey), 89, 91
Curtis, J. L., 135

Damon, W., 30
Dandelion Adventures (Kite), 54
Davis, J., 71
Demonstrations, 44
*Developmentally Appropriate Practice in Early
    Childhood Programs* (Bredekamp and
    Copple), 40
Dewey, John, 4, 5, 19, 30, 40
Diehn, G., 97
Dighe, J., 14
Documenting children's learning
  children as scientists experiences and, 85
  healthy bodies experiences and, 141
  how toys work experiences and, 92
  insects/small animals experiences and, 73
  rocks/minerals experiences and, 114
  seeds/plants experiences and, 55, 57
  senses experiences and, 128
  water experiences and, 102
Doing What Scientists Do (Doris), 81
Dooley, N., 135, 137
Doris, E., 81
Dorros, A., 67
Down Comes the Rain (Branley), 97, 101
Down Comes the Rain (Hale), 97, 101
Drop in My Drink, The (Hooper), 97
Drop of Water, A (Wick), 98, 99

Early primary grades
  healthy bodies experiences and, 140–141
  insects/small animals experiences and, 72–73
  rocks/minerals experiences and, 113–114
  seeds/plants experiences and, 55–56
  senses experiences and, 127–128
  water experiences and, 101–102

Ears Are for Hearing (Showers), 121
Earth: The Water Planet (Gartrell, Crowder and Callister), 97
Earth at Hand (Callister and Stroud), 109
Earth science and physical setting, 13, 42. *See also* Rocks/minerals experiences; Water experiences
Eating (Ganeri), 135
Ecological approach, 30
Edible Pyramid, The (Leedy), 136, 139
Education, U.S. Department of, 52, 56, 111
Elementary Science Methods (Martin), 97
Energy sources, 89–91
Environments and life cycles
    field activities and, 35
    healthy bodies experiences and, 141
    insects/small animals experiences, 70
Equipment
    health and safety considerations for, 10–11, 26
    math activities and, 24
    outdoor learning environments and, 25
Equity. *See* Inclusion
Evaluating children's learning, 4, 6. *See also* Assessment
Everybody Needs a Rock (Baylor), 13, 109
Everyone Cooks Rice (Dooley), 135, 137
Everything Grows (Raffi), 51
Exercise and Your Health (Powell), 135
Explore Your World (National Science Teachers Association), 109
Eyewitness Explorers (Parker), 109

Field activities, 30–38
    basic guidelines for, 33–34
    community resources and, 30, 32–33, 35–36
    home involvement and, 34, 36–38
    inclusion and, 33
    inside school building, 32
    intergenerational programs and, 35
    neighborhood resources and, 32–33, 35–36
    outside school grounds, 31–32
    safety tips for, 34
    seeds/plants experiences and, 56
Firsthand experiences, 40, 44–45. *See also* Field activities; Hands-on learning
Fit for Life (Parsons), 135
Five Senses (Rius, Parramon and Puig), 121
Five Senses, The (Hewitt), 121
Fleischman, P., 67
Florian, D., 51, 55
Food guide pyramid, 137
Forum on Early Childhood Science, Mathematics, and Technology Education, 4
Fossils Tell of Long Ago (Aliki), 109
Fostering a Sense of Wonder During the Early Childhood Years (Wilson), 51
From Caterpillar to Butterfly (Herligman), 67
From Seed to Plant (Gibbons), 51

Ganeri, A., 135
Gans, Roma, 112
Garden (Maass), 51
Gartrell, J. E., 97
Geology (Stotsky), 110
Germs Make Me Sick (Berger), 135
Gibbons, G., 51, 141
Glaser, L., 67
Grassy, J., 51, 67
Graves, K., 51
Great Kapok Tree, The (Cherry), 141
Gregory the Terrible Eater (Sharmat), 136
Grolnick, W. S., 36

Hale, J. G., 97, 101
Hands-on learning
    children's literature and, 16
    conceptual learning and, 40
    field activities and, 35
    insects/small animals experiences and, 68
    science experiences and, 4
    science subject matter and, 41
Harlan, J. D., 13, 23, 30
Harrison, G., 67
Hausherr, R., 135
Health. *See* Healthy bodies experiences; Safety and health considerations
Healthy bodies experiences, 134–143
    assessment and, 138, 142
    documenting children's learning, 141
    early primary grades and, 140–141
    goals and objectives, 134–135
    home involvement and, 136–138
    indoor/outdoor activities for, 138–140
    key concepts, 134
    literary resources, 135–136
    observation form, 143
    reflection and, 140
    sample evaluation form, 142
    supplies for, 135–136
    teaching strategies for, 134–138
Hearing-impaired children, 11, 120, 123
Helm, J. H., 4
Helping Your Child Learn Science (Paulu), 52, 56, 69, 111
Herligman, D., 67
Hewitt, S., 121
Hoban, R., 135
Hoban, T., 136
Hoberman, M. A., 136
Hofman, H., 10, 26, 40, 41
Home involvement
    assessment of prior knowledge and, 43
    children as scientists experiences and, 81–82
    field activities and, 34, 36–38
    healthy bodies experiences and, 136–138
    how toys work experiences and, 89, 93

Home involvement—*Cont.*
   insects/small animals experiences and, 68–69,
      74–75
   rocks/minerals experiences and, 110–111, 115
   safety and health considerations, 11, 136–138
   science experiences and, 30
   seeds/plants experiences and, 52, 55, 58–60
   senses experiences and, 122, 129
   water experiences and, 98
Hooper, M., 97
Horenstein, S., 109
How Birds Build Their Amazing Homes
    (Robinson), 67
How Do I Know It's Yucky? (Cromwell), 121
How Do We Feel and Touch? (Ballard), 121
How Do We Taste and Smell? (Ballard), 121
How toys work experiences, 88–93
   assessment and, 89
   children's literature and, 89
   documenting children's learning, 92
   energy sources and, 88, 89–91
   goals and objectives, 88
   home involvement and, 89, 93
   key concepts, 88
   parent letter, 93
   supplies for, 88–89
   teaching strategies for, 88–89
   vibrations and, 88, 92
Hughes, Meredith Sayles, 51
Hughes, Tom, 51
Human Body, The (Miller), 121
Human Body, The (Parker), 135

I Am a Rock (Marzollo), 109, 114
I Am Water (Marzollo), 97
Icky Bug Book, The (Palotta), 67
If You Find a Rock (Christian), 109, 110
I Hear, I See, I Touch (Oxenbury), 121
Inclusion. *See also* Children with special needs
   field activities and, 33
   indoor learning environment and, 10, 11–12, 19
   planning for, 11–12
   science subject matter and, 41
   senses experiences and, 11, 123
   teaching strategies and, 7
Indoor learning environment, 10–19
   art centers and, 14–15
   block areas and, 17
   book and library centers and, 15–16
   centers of interest and, 12–18
   components of, 10–12
   computer stations and, 18
   inclusion and, 10, 11–12, 19
   manipulatives areas and, 17
   music areas and, 17
   quiet spaces and, 18
   science areas and, 13–14
   sociodramatic play areas and, 16–17

   teacher's role and, 11, 18–19, 26
   water and sand areas and, 17
   woodworking centers and, 15
Informal learning experiences, 7
Insect Book, The (Zakowski), 68
Insects (Wilston), 67
Insects and small animals
   classroom pets, 71–72
   field activities and, 35, 36
   indoor learning environment and, 14, 66
   outdoor learning environment and, 23–24, 66
   outside school building and, 32, 66
Insects/small animals experiences, 66–77
   assessment and, 69, 77
   children's literature and, 67–68, 71
   documenting children's learning, 73
   early primary grades and, 72–73
   environments and life cycles, 70
   goals and objectives for, 66–67
   home involvement and, 68–69, 74–75
   key concepts, 66
   observation and, 66, 69–71
   observation form, 76
   parent letters, 74–75
   process skills and, 66
   reflection and, 72
   supplies for, 67–68
   teaching strategies for, 66–69
Integrated curriculum, 13, 15, 23, 33
Integrated learning, 4
Intergenerational programs, 35
Investigations, and children as scientists
    experiences, 80, 84–85
I Scream, You Scream (Morrison), 135
Is It Alive? (Graves), 51

Jeunessa, G., 97
Joyful Noise (Fleischman), 67

Katz, L., 4, 19
Keene, C., 51, 67
Kids Discover (Sands), 121
Kilmer, S. J., 10, 26, 40, 41
Kite, L. Patricia, 54
Kittinger, J. S., 109
Kneidel, S., 67
Kramer, D., 67
Krautwurst, T., 97

Learning environment. *See* Indoor learning
    environment; Outdoor learning environment
Leedy, L., 136, 139
Let's Go Rock Collecting (Gans), 112
Life science and living environment, 13, 32, 42.
    See also Insects/small animals experiences;
    Seeds/plants experiences
Lionni, L., 89, 90, 109, 112
Liquid Explorations (Agler), 97

Listening Walk, The (Showers), 121, 122
Listen . . . What Do You Hear? (Wood and Rye), 121
Literary resources
 book and library centers and, 15
 children as scientists experiences, 81
 enhancing firsthand experiences with, 44
 healthy bodies experiences, 135–136
 how toys work experiences, 89
 insects/small animals experiences, 67–68
 rocks/minerals experiences, 109–110
 seeds/plants experiences, 51, 54–55
 senses experiences and, 120–121
 water experiences, 97–98
Look at Rocks, A (Kittinger), 109
Louglin, C., 11
Lowery, L., 4, 6
Lynch, E. C., 15

Maass, Robert, 51
McMillan, B., 121, 122
Magic Schoolbus, The (Cole), 135, 141
Magic School Bus Wet All Over, The (Relf), 97, 101
Mallory, B. L., 11, 12
Mandy (Booth), 121, 124
Manipulatives areas, 17
Marcon, R., 36
Martin, B., Jr., 121
Martin, D. J., 97
Marzollo, J., 97, 109, 114
Math activities, 24
Max Found Two Sticks (Pinkney), 89, 92
Miller, J., 121
Mister Roger's First Experience Book (Rogers), 67
Montessori, Maria, 5
More Science Through Children's Literature (Butzow and Butzow), 97
Morris, A., 136, 140
Morrison, L., 135
Moss, L., 89, 92
Moving (Ganeri), 135
Museums
 field activities and, 33, 36
 home minimuseums, 38, 54
 seeds/plants experiences and, 56
 teacher strategies and, 43
Music areas, 17
My Five Senses (Aliki), 121, 122

National Academy of Sciences, 50, 52
National Association for the Education of Young Children, 4, 43
National Audubon Society First Field Guide: Wild Flowers (Rockwell), 51
National Audubon Society First Field Guide to Mammals (Grassy and Keene), 51, 67
National Research Council, 4, 5, 6, 7, 11, 13, 30, 40, 41, 42, 43, 44, 45, 50

National Science Education Standards (National Academy of Sciences), 50
National Science Education Standards (National Research Council), 4, 5, 6, 7, 11, 13, 30, 40, 41, 42, 43, 50
National Science Teachers Association, 37, 43, 50, 52, 109, 121
Natural History of the Senses (Ackerman), 120
Natural resources, 35
Natural sciences, 13
Neighborhood resources, 32–33, 35–36, 43
Nests, 70–71
New, R. S., 12
NSTA Pathways to the Science Standards: Elementary School Edition (Lowery), 4
Nutrition, 134, 137
Nutrition (Patent), 135

Observation
 children as scientists experiences and, 80, 82–83
 field experiences and, 34
 firsthand experiences and, 44
 insects/small animals experiences and, 66, 69–71
 outdoor learning environment and, 22
 rocks/minerals experiences and, 108
 science subject matter and, 41
 seeds/plants experiences and, 53, 56, 61
 senses experiences and, 122
 water experiences and, 96
On My Beach There Are Many Pebbles (Lionni), 109, 112
On the Spot (Royston), 113
Organizing children's experiences, 42. *See also* Reflection
Our Wet World (Collard), 51
Outdoor learning environment, 22–27
 art activities and, 24
 benefits of, 22–23
 math activities and, 24
 physical activities and, 25
 safety and health considerations and, 26
 science/nature discovery areas and, 13, 23–24
 senses experiences and, 22, 123
 space planning and, 23–26
 teacher's role and, 25–27
Outstanding Science Trade Books for Children-1999, The, 50, 67
Oxenbury, H., 121

Palotta, J., 67
Parental involvement. *See* Home involvement
Parent observation, 37
Parker, N. W., 67
Parker, S., 109, 135
Parramon, J. M., 121
Parsons, A., 135
Patent, A., 135

Paulu, Nancy, 52, 56, 69, 111
Peer interaction, 45
Pellant, C., 109
Personal/social perspectives and human organism,
        42. *See also* Healthy bodies experiences;
        Senses experiences
Physical activities, 25
Physical disabilities, 11
Physical science, physical setting and designed
        world, 13, 42. *See also* Children as scientists
        experiences; How toys work experiences
Piaget, Jean, 5, 23, 30, 40
Picture Book of Helen Keller, A (Adler), 128
Picture book of Louis Braille, A (Adler), 128
Pines, M., 121
Pinkney, J. B., 89, 92
Plants. *See also* Seeds/plants experiences
        indoor learning environment and, 14
        outdoor learning environment and, 24
        outside school building and, 32
Pledger, M., 97
Polar Bear, Polar Bear, What Do You Hear?
        (Martin and Carle), 121
Powell, D. R., 36
Powell, J., 135
Preoperational stage, 5, 40
Prinz, M., 109
Problem-solving techniques, 7
Problems as Possibilities (Torp and Sage), 109
Process skills, 50, 53–54, 66
Project Approach, 4
Puig, J. J., 121
Pyramid Cookbook, The (Baird), 135

Questions
        children as scientists experiences and, 80, 83–84
        enhancing firsthand experiences with, 44
Quiet spaces, 18

Raffi, 51
"Rain" (Stevenson), 101
Recycle! (Gibbons), 141
Reflection
        field experiences and, 31
        healthy bodies experiences and, 140
        insects/small animals experiences and, 72
        quiet spaces and, 18
        rocks/minerals experiences and, 113
        science subject matter and, 41
        seeds/plants experiences and, 55
        senses experiences and, 127
        teaching strategies and, 7
        water experiences and, 101
Relf, P., 97, 101
Rey, M., 89, 91
Rius, M., 121
Rivkin, M. S., 13, 23, 26, 30, 32
Robbins, Ken, 51

Robinson, W. W., 67
Rocks and Fossils (Rook, Coenraads and
        Busbey), 110
Rocks/minerals experiences, 108–117
        assessment and, 111, 117
        documenting children's learning, 114
        early primary grades and, 113–114
        goals and objectives, 108
        home involvement, 110–111, 115
        indoor/outdoor activities for, 111–113
        key concepts, 108
        literary resources, 109–110
        observation form, 116
        parent letter, 115
        reflection and, 113
        supplies for, 109–110
        teaching strategies for, 108–110
Rocks and Minerals (Pellant), 109
Rocks Tell Stories (Horenstein), 109
Rockwell, Anne, 51
Rogers, F., 67
Rook, D., 110
Rosegrant, T., 45
Royston, Angela, 113
Rye, J., 121

Safety and health considerations
        equipment and, 10–11, 26
        field activities and, 34
        home involvement, 11, 136–138
        how toys work experiences and, 88
        indoor learning environment and, 10–11, 13
        outdoor learning environment and, 26
        senses experiences and, 122
Sage, S., 109
Sand areas, 17, 23, 111
Sandeman, A., 135, 136, 139
Sands, S., 121
Sandved, K., 68
Scarborough, K., 68
Schoon, S., 44
Science & Children (journal), 121
Science
        defined, 41
        as subject matter, 41, 43
Science for All Americans (American Association
        for the Advancement of Science), 4
Science Book of the Senses, The (Ardley), 120
Science Books and Films (American Association
        for the Advancement of Science), 109
Science Crafts for Kids (Diehn and Krautwurst), 97
Science experiences. *See also* Children as
        scientists experiences; Field activities;
        Healthy bodies experiences; How toys work
        experiences; Insects/small animals
        experiences; Rocks/minerals experiences;
        Seeds/plants experiences; Senses
        experiences; Water experiences

content integrity and meaning of, 5
content standards and, 4–5
expanding/extending of, 44–45
home involvement and, 30
organization of, 42
Science/nature discovery areas, 13–14, 23–24, 36, 56
Sciencing, 41
Seeds/plants experiences, 50–63
  arts and crafts and, 55
  assessment and, 52, 62
  children's literature and, 51, 54–55
  documenting children's learning, 55, 57
  early primary grades and, 55–56
  evaluation form, 62
  goals and objectives, 50
  home involvement and, 52, 55, 58–60
  key concepts and, 50
  observation and, 53, 56, 61
  observation form, 61
  parent letters, 58–60
  process skills and, 50, 53–54
  reflection and, 55
  root viewer instruction form, 63
  sample science exhibit and party invitation, 60
  supplies for, 50–52
  teacher strategies for, 50–52
Seefeldt, C., 11, 12, 33, 35, 50
Seeing, Smelling, and Hearing the World (Pines), 121
See for Yourself Series: Touch Smell and Taste, Seeing, and Hearing (Walpole), 121
Senses experiences, 120–131
  assessment and, 122–123, 131
  children with special needs and, 120, 123
  documenting children's learning, 128
  early primary grades and, 127–128
  goals and objectives, 120
  home involvement and, 122, 129
  inclusion and, 11, 123
  key concepts, 120
  literary resources, 120–121
  observation form, 130
  odor and, 124–125
  outdoor learning environment and, 22, 123
  parent letter, 129
  reflection and, 127
  sample evaluation form, 131
  sight and, 126–127
  smell and, 124–125
  sound and, 123–124
  supplies for, 120–121
  taste and, 126
  teaching strategies for, 120–121
  touch and, 125–126
Sense Suspense (McMillan), 121, 122
Seven Silly Eaters, The (Hoberman), 136
Shade, D. D., 18

Sharmat, M., 136
Showers, P., 121, 122, 136, 139
Sight, sense of, 126–127
Simon and Schuster's Guide to Rocks and Minerals (Prinz), 109
Site preview, and field activities, 33
Slowiaczek, M. L., 36
Smell, sense of, 124–125
Sociodramatic play areas, 16–17
Sound, 123–124
Sources of energy, 89–91
Space planning, 23–26
Space sciences, 13
Spiders Nest (Scarborough), 68
Stevenson, D. L., 36
Stevenson, Robert Louis, 101
Stotsky, S., 110
Stroud, S., 109
Suina, J., 11
Sunflowers for Tina (Baldwin), 51, 55
Swick, K. J., 35

Taste, sense of, 126
Teachable moment, 7
Teacher's role
  indoor learning environment and, 11, 18–19, 26
  outdoor learning environment and, 25–27
Teaching strategies
  for children as scientists experiences, 80–82
  community resources and, 30, 33
  field activities and, 32–33, 34
  firsthand experiences and, 44–45
  group and individual teaching, 4
  for healthy bodies experiences, 134–138
  home involvement and, 36–38
  for how toys work experiences, 88–89
  for insects/small animals experiences, 66–69
  for rocks/minerals experiences, 108–110
  science as inquiry and, 41
  for science learning, 6–7, 50
  science subject matter and, 41, 43
  for seeds/plants experiences, 50–52
  for senses experiences, 120–121
  for water experiences, 96–98
Tiny Seed, The (Carle), 51, 54
Torp, L., 109
Touch, sense of, 125–126
Touch . . . What Do You Feel? (Wood and Willey), 121
Traser, L., 41

Van Zutphen, C., 14
Vegetable Garden (Florian), 51, 55
Very Busy Spider, The (Carle), 67
Very Hungry Caterpillar, The (Carle), 67
Very Quiet Cricket, The (Carle), 67
Visitors, and field activities, 35
Visually impaired children, 11, 120, 123

Vocabulary
  enhancing firsthand experiences with, 44
  healthy bodies experiences and, 143
  insects/small animals experiences, 66, 70, 72
  rocks/minerals experiences and, 109
  seeds/plants experiences and, 53, 54, 56
  senses experiences and, 130
Vygotsky, Lev, 5, 19, 26, 30, 44

Walpole, B., 121
Water (Jeunessa), 97
Water and sand areas, 17, 23, 111
Water cycle, 96
Water experiences, 96–105
  assessment and, 99, 103
  documenting children's learning, 102
  early primary grades and, 101–102
  goals and objectives, 96–97
  home involvement and, 98
  indoor/outdoor activities for, 99–101
  key concepts, 96
  literary resources, 97–98
  observation and, 96
  observation form, 105
  parent letter, 104
  reflection, 101
  supplies for, 98
  teaching strategies and, 96–98
Water Matters (Crowder and Cain), 97
Water, Water Everywhere (Berger and Berger),
  97, 101
Weiss, E., 97
Wenner, G., 41

What Food is This? (Hausherr), 135
What is the World Made of (Zoehfeld), 81
What Makes It Rain (Brandt), 97
Wheelchair accessibility, 11
When I Was Little (Curtis), 135
Why I Cough, Sneeze, Shiver, Hiccup, & Yawn
  (Berger), 135
Wick, W., 98, 99
Wild, Wild Sunflower Child Anna (Carlstrom),
  51, 54
Willey, L., 121
Wilson, R. A., 12, 22, 24, 32
Wilson, Ruth, 51
Wilston, C., 67
Winsler, A., 19, 30
Wonderful Worms (Glaser), 67
Wood, N., 121
Woodworking centers, 15
Wright, J. L., 18
Wright, J. R., 67

You Breathe In, You Breathe Out (Adler), 135, 138
You Can't Make a Move Without Your Muscles
  (Showers), 136, 139
Youniss, J., 30
Your Insides (Cole), 135

Zakowski, C., 68
Zin, Zin, Zin! A Violin (Moss), 89, 92
Zoehfeld, K. W., 81
Zone of proximal development, 19, 44
Zoos, 35–36, 66